In Artists' Homes

In Artists' Homes

By Roberta Kimmel

•

**Text by Roberta Kimmel
with Edith Newhall**

**Photographs by Kari Haavisto
Design by Judy Schiern Hecker**

Clarkson Potter/Publishers
New York

For Helen and Maurice, together again

AUTHOR'S NOTE: All paintings are oil on canvas unless otherwise noted.

Published by Clarkson N. Potter, Inc., 201 East 50th Street, New York, New York 10022. Member of the Crown Publishing Group.

CLARKSON N. POTTER, POTTER, and colophon are trademarks of Clarkson N. Potter, Inc.

Manufactured in Japan

Library of Congress Cataloging-in-Publication Data
Kimmel, Roberta.
In artists' homes: the living spaces of contemporary artists/by Roberta Kimmel; photographs by Kari Haavisto.
Includes index.
1. Artists—Homes and haunts—United States. 2. Interior decoration—United States—History—20th century. I. Title.
NK2445.3.A78K55   1992
747'.08'87—dc20   92-8022
ISBN 0-517-57788-7

10 9 8 7 6 5 4 3 2 1

First Edition

acknowledgments

One lazy August afternoon in the country, I mentioned to old friends that I had an idea for a book, and Ruth Randall suggested that I write a description of an artist's home. So began the passage from idea to realization, with Ruth's guidance from the beginning sentence down to the very last period. There are not enough words to thank you, Ruth, for your friendship, intelligence, never-ending patience, and support. Thank you Alyne Model for all those times I stumbled over ideas, and you offered much-needed encouragement.

A book is borne out of a compelling ambition, long hours, and labors of love, but without a large support system to draw from, the book would have been an impossible task. Thank you to each friend who added his or her special touch: Alice Adam and Michael Pado, Aviva and Jacob Baal Teshuva, Jeanne and Zachary Buchalter, Mary Randolph Carter and Howard Berg, Moishe and R. O. Blechman, Sherrie and Gary Citron, Corinne Curry and Harold Farberman, Olga and Vic Firth, Susan Franklin, Valerie Hemingway, Jacques Kaplan, Dorothy Kay, Robert Monroe, Walter and Linda Rothschild, and Eleanor Schwartz.

I wish to thank the Clarkson Potter staff, whose ceaseless efforts made it all possible: Pamela Krauss for her rare gift of turning the perfect phrase; Carol Southern for her faith in this work; Howard Klein for his acute, expert art direction; and Katie Workman for her aid. Thank you to Anne Edelstein for her excellent literary acumen; Judy Schiern Hecker for her wonderfully fresh design; Edith Newhall for her contributions to the text; and Robin Howard for sharing her incredible vocabulary.

Most important, thank you Kari Haavisto for your incredibly intuitive, sensitive photographs. Thank you Elizabeth Gaynor for the ease with which you handled the photograph schedules.

But it is to the artists that I owe the most gratitude, for the visits to the artists' homes were exciting, exhilarating experiences made even more pleasurable by their enlightened interviews, gracious hospitality, and generosity. I am deeply appreciative to each one of you for your time, support, and dedication to this project: Peter Alexander, Carol Anthony, Naomi and Stephen Antonakos, Corice and Armand Arman, Katie and Charles Arnoldi, Jennifer Bartlett, Ed Baynard, Sondra and Jack Beal, Larry Bell, Karen and Lynda Benglis and Anand Sarabhai, Christi and Billy Al Bengston, Mel Bochner and Lizbeth Marano, Fernando Botero and Sophia Vari, Anthony Caro, Chuck Close, Jane and Robert Cottingham, Robert Dash, David Deutsch, Laddie John Dill, Richard Estes and José Saenz, Janet Fish and Charles Parnass, Helen Frankenthaler, Jane Freilicher, Ilse Getz and Gibson Danes, Shana and Ralph Goings, Nancy Graves, Jan Hashey and Yasuo Minagawa, Al Held, Ada and Alex Katz, Anita and Conrad Marca-Relli, Agnes Martin, David McDermott, Peter McGough and Jeffrey Gasparini, Nabil Nahas, Lowell Nesbitt, Ken Noland, Alfonso Ossorio y Yangco and Edward Dragon, Izhar Patkin, Edith and George Rickey, Dorothea Rockburne, Carol and Paul Sarkisian, George Segal, Joel Shapiro and Ellen Phalen, Ron Stein, Michael Steiner, Tavlos, Shelia and Neil Welliver, Claire and Tom Wesselmann, and Jack Youngerman.

To all the artists' studio assistants who were of invaluable help, I would like to extend my thanks: Gretchen Corners, Kathy Hofmeyer, Celia Johnson, Wayne Osborne, Lois Rodin, Mike Russell, Jane Samuels, Charlotte Shusterman, Cynthia Siu, Maureen St. Onge, and Eric Wolf. And also, thank you to the artists' galleries for their cooperation and information. To Klaus Kertess, Miani Johnson, and Paula Cooper I give my heartfelt thanks again for the joy of working with you all those many years ago.

Finally, my love and thanks to my family: Dick, Ronna, Stephanie, Alan, Joel, Sue, Beth, Andrew, Evi, Mel, but most of all to my husband, Richard Cohn. And a silent thank you to Lee Krasner, Helene and Erich Cohn, and above all, to my beloved parents.

The living room entry sports part of a hat and rifle collection at Larry Bell's home; at left, his 1991 work on paper.

contents

The Home as Inspiration

The Home as Retreat

An artist's sensibility leaves its imprint everywhere. The home, especially, offers not only a glimpse into the aesthetic that shapes an artist's work, but often the inspiration behind it. When the same decision making and thought process an artist uses to create a work of art continues beyond the studio into his or her home, the result is a space that reflects—sometimes directly, sometimes more subtly—the spirit, feeling, and character of the artist's work.

As a young woman I often stayed in New York City with Lee Krasner, widow of Jackson Pollock and my aunt through marriage. It was there that I first recognized how distinctively different an artist's environment can be, how proportion was more important than decoration. The furnishings were simple yet elegant: intricately woven wicker chairs, marble-topped burled maple side-

Tubes of translucent fiberglass enclose a trio of fluorescent tubes in Jennifer Bartlett's New York duplex.

boards, an Art Nouveau abalone shell lamp, and the sunny, high-ceilinged rooms were separated by tall columned archways. Two narrow black-and-white Pollock paintings hung almost floor-to-ceiling on either side of the fireplace; a painting by Krasner covered the entire opposite wall. It was an easy, natural setting that invited curiosity and inspired creativity along with good companionship and always interesting conversation.

Aunt Lee was my mentor and guide into the New York art world, and with her I visited many artists in their homes: from Adolph Gottlieb, who traded art for furniture with his friend Herman Miller, to the converted stable-turned-home of Anita and Conrad Marca-Relli, to Edward Dragon and Alfonso Ossorio y Yangco's exotic East Hampton estate crowded with paintings (Ossorio's, as well as works by Dubuffet, Pol-

introduction

lock, and others), furniture, and mementos both rare and ordinary mixed together like a richly patterned mosaic. These were vital homes, unconventional yet gracious, where artists spent their nonworking hours in much the same way as they do today: relaxing with family, tending their gardens, helping their children with homework, cooking dinner for friends.

Artists' living quarters are as vastly different as the works they create. For some, their home is a showcase for art as well as artifacts from distant cultures. For others, objects that inspire or give meaning to the artists' work or lives are the focal point. Homes can be a respite from the world of art, a getaway to renew the spirit, and I also found entire houses that could be perceived as works of art themselves. Whether a cottage in Maine, a high-tech glass and concrete structure in New Mexico,

Stickley and Thonet furniture mixes with columns in Dorothea Rockburne's New York loft, **above** *and* **overleaf.**

an updated thirties bungalow in California, or a nineteenth-century farmhouse in upstate New York, these dwellings are invariably filled with the small touches or visionary gestures that identify them as the homes of artists.

The line between art and reality is often a fine one. The first time I wanted to make a telephone call from Man Ray's Paris studio-home, I first had to determine whether the object on a shelf crammed with his Dada ready-mades, photographs, and objects was in fact a working telephone (it was): His entire environment was a work of art. Today, Janet Fish's Vermont landscape contains images of gardens, ponds, and whirligigs that are interchangeable with her highly detailed paintings, just as the pastoral surroundings of Sondra and Jack Beal's Oneonta waterfalls provide scenes for the idealized realism of his canvases.

Invention and imagination often collide, blurring the distinction between art and furniture. Arman transforms violin scrolls and neck parts not only into works of art but also into table legs and carpet motifs. In Tavlos's house, almost everything echoes the artist's outrageous palette of intense Southwestern colors and the zigzag patterns that border his paintings.

During my travels I saw that the artist's home is made to serve multiple roles; most important, it is a place where the artist can live with and view the work outside of his or her studio. Both Anthony Caro and George Rickey install their sculptures in parklike greenery to get a read-out of how they interact with the environment. Dorothea Rockburne hangs recent paintings in the whiteness of her relaxed living space, where she can watch how the changing light affects work that was made

Organic foods and natural light are fundamental ingredients of McDermott and McGough's lifestyles.

in the studio's shadowless lighting. Finding a different perspective gives the artist the opportunity to discover new ideas, for the pattern of those shadows may appear in a future work.

In the hands of artists, materials take on fresh life, too. Again and again I found the studio aesthetic transplanted to the home. Laddie John Dill has incorporated the same materials he uses in his studio into his Santa Monica house, and in Taos, Larry Bell has introduced the iridescent glass ovals of his sculpture into his kitchen cabinet doors. Charles Arnoldi fabricates furniture along with his sculpture at his foundry, bringing both into his home along with other materials used in his work.

When renovating old houses, artists are likely to reclaim the past in a more personal, emotional way. Neil Welliver accomplished his skillful restoration by rebuilding his home plank by plank, beam by beam, updating conveniences while retaining the original character. Color, too, changes the feeling of an older house; Jan Hashey's farmhouse affectionately recalls its heritage through hues associated with early American practicality.

Artists have always reinvented their environments, creating new archetypes when the old ones no longer sufficed. Before the turn of this century, landscape painter Henry Ward Ranger found he could not afford to maintain both an apartment and studio space, nor did he have a place to show his work. He set out to design a building that would fulfill an artist's requirements: living quarters, work space, and exhibition space. The result was the first cooperative studio-apartment building, built in New York City in 1901, with double-height rooms and gigantic north windows. Today, artists have revitalized entire neighborhoods, primarily neglected industrial districts, in search of such spaces: SoHo and TriBeCa in New York, South Beach in Miami, Venice in California, the Third Ward in my hometown, Milwaukee, and others across the country.

Twig fencing encloses R. O. Blechman's vegetable garden in Columbia County, New York.

But perhaps the most compelling quality an artist imparts to his or her home is a sense of mystery. Nowhere was this more explicitly conveyed than in the New Mexico home of Agnes Martin: Her undaunted spirit and clear thinking made this one of the most thought-provoking visits for me. By stripping away all but the essentials, Martin has created an environment that made me recall an Albert Einstein quotation, "The most beautiful thing we can experience is the mysterious. It is the source of all true art and science."

Roberta Kimmel

iN THE CATALOGUE for an exhibition of Dorothea Rockburne's paintings, art dealer André Emmerich apologized for failing to provide a place for the gallery goer to sit while viewing the show, ex-

The New York City pied-à-terre of artists Sophia Vari and Fernando Botero features his sculpture.

plaining that sitting in a very comfortable armchair was surely the best way to look at art. His point is well taken, for to respond

The Home as

to art, a relaxed posture is the most conducive one. For artists, leisurely observation is a necessity, especially when their studios are in a factory or foundry. Taking a painting or sculpture into living environments, where conditions for viewing are close to ideal, makes their homes in a sense a laboratory. Because artists have firm opinions regarding how art should be displayed and viewed, observing their homes can be a lesson in the combination of energy, imagination, and improvisation required to create a situation that integrates art and the practicalities of everyday living. Stephen Antonakos's white, many-windowed SoHo loft is the perfect place for observing the way **Gallery** in which his colorful neon sculptures respond to changing light. A few blocks away, Nancy Graves's work is juxtaposed with artifacts collected during her travels: Tibetan and New Guinean pieces reside in the kitchen;

just beyond, a room reserved for recent paintings and sculptures is devoid of furniture except for a solo chair. Some of her sculptures are freestanding, others jut out from their background

Roy Campbell's sculpture hangs in Santa Fe artists Carol and Paul Sarkisian's home.

paintings, but the setting allows for unobstructed viewing.

SoHo residents Ellen Phelan and Joel Shapiro's art display includes Shapiro's 1987–1988 plaster sculpture.

Painters Nabil Nahas and Mel Bochner live on the same street in TriBeCa, and although both combine the aesthetics of their revolving collections with their art, the results are as disparate as their work.

Nahas clusters objects in a somewhat casual but elegant manner, while Bochner and his wife, sculptor Lizbeth Marano, display their art and artifacts against vivid-colored backgrounds. Lynda Benglis has both representational and abstract art in her East Hampton home, but most of the pieces she collects share

An assortment of plaster sculpture parts awaiting final assembly in George Segal's New Jersey farmhouse.

the unexpected materials that characterize her own sculpture. But in each of these homes, the artist's desire to view his or her work objectively is quickly communicated. Their living

A former dairy barn near Woodstock was transformed into Al Held's studio.

quarters are clearly places to experiment, whether by reinforcing ideas through the juxtaposition of color, light, and object, or by the introduction of entirely new concepts.

the rhythm of light

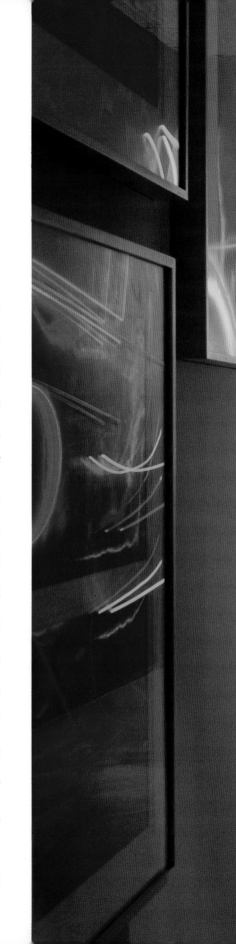

White and more white on floors, walls, ceilings, furniture, tiles, and cabinets makes Stephen Antonakos's loft a setting that clearly reflects his Greek heritage. The space also functions as a laboratory in which the artist's abstract neon sculptures, constantly transformed by the rhythm of light reflecting off one pristine surface after another, can be observed and experienced. "In daylight, the exposed neon tubes seem very concrete," says Antonakos. "You see the glass tubing and a very hot line of neon in it. But as evening falls and there is less auxiliary light, the colored glow of the neon gradually comes out. The work is made with an understanding of the gradation throughout the daily cycle. It is to be completed by the viewer, by the viewer's imagination." ● Antonakos was only four when his family immigrated to New York, but an

Stephen Antonakos

PREVIOUS PAGE: *Neon for the Studio, 1991, illuminates a wall hung with photographs of Antonakos's installations and gleams on the Varathane-painted floor.* **ABOVE:** *On a Gilbert Rohde chrome end table, a glass dish holds round and square dice, with and without dots.* **RIGHT:** *The artist says he is "too close" to draw comparisons, but the similarities between his work and that of Gerrit Thomas Rietveld, the twenty-nine-year-old cabinetmaker whose 1918 Red/Blue Chair (seen opposite) marked the emergence of the de Stijl movement, are striking. Here, behind Rietveld's 1919 High Back Chairs, is the artist's* Ancient Sparta, *1988, in white gold leaf.*

impression of the small Greek village in which he was born has remained firmly etched in his memory. The artist and his wife, Naomi, have lived in SoHo since 1963 and share their home with their daughter, Evangelia. The loft's generous expanse of open space and flooding light give it a distinctly Mediterranean feeling. By chance, the loft already had an arch that was reminiscent of Greek architecture, and the couple focused the kitchen area around this curve, leaving exposed, rough bricks to contrast with the smooth white counters and cabinets. To repeat the curved space, Antonakos made a broad white table with rounded corners, which is supported by shaped pipes underneath.

A small cluster of white leather furniture and Rietveld chairs form another area across from the kitchen. At the center is a low table designed by Antonakos, which displays various remembrances of visits to Greece: fragile textiles, thin bracelets, old tiles. Arrayed atop one of the black-and-chrome tables are Greek worry beads in amber, ivory, and silver. These small but intense areas of incidence are another nod to Antonakos's background: "If you go into a Greek chapel you see all the white, soft surfaces of the walls, and

LEFT AND BELOW: *"What you have as a child, you must eventually find again and make your own: that is the broad outline of what has happened here,"* says Antonakos. *In the angular seating area with Zographos's leather furniture, the artist's 1983 glass-covered wood table showcases a mélange of Greek objects and two of daughter Evangelia's shaped wire flower holders; behind,* Untitled (for Budd Bishop), *1986.*

LEFT AND ABOVE: *Proportioned to the area as well as to himself, Antonakos created* Neon Table No. 2, *1990, with two slanting planes that relate to its diagonal placement in his drawing studio. The desk, which anchors the space, is constructed from galvanized sheet metal, neon, and glass. Evangelia's portrait sits on top; at left,* Mistra, *1988, in white Varathane paint on wood; at right,* Resurrection, *1989, in gold leaf.*

then you see the icons," says Naomi. "They are dark: black, red, gold. They are concentrated and intense. Their placement is echoed, for instance, in the way Stephen has hung drawings up in corners near the ceiling, off-balance: That feels close to the way icons are sometimes placed at home and in the little chapels in Greece."

But by and large the walls and surfaces have been left bare of embellishment, the better to reflect and bathe in the glow of the artist's blazing pieces. Antonakos's work should be seen from different perspectives, and for this reason the artist has kept the space open. Some walls stop just short of the ceilings, and even the chairs have a see-through quality that relates to the spatial nature of his work.

Whether it is a pile of books, a table full of little items, or the placement of rings of clear red neon on a painted canvas, there is a kinetic exchange and strong emotional content in each area of the Antonakos home, a specific way of arranging art and objects with a hard Greek intensity.

ABOVE: *A large bathroom houses a wall of travel mementos made into framed collages and* **A Pink Neon with a Pink Painting, 1983.** RIGHT: *The kitchen is a study in contrasts: behind smooth counters, an exposed brick arch was kept rough as a reminder of the stone arches found in the Peloponnisos; the opacity of his 1989 ceramic sculptures is stark against the transparency of* **Neon Table No. 1,** *1986.*

lively minimalism

Few artists have experimented with as many mediums as Lynda Benglis. From her early poured-latex pieces that appear to ooze across the floor to more recent pleated metal sculptures that billow out from the wall, Benglis has turned process into a kind of sorcery. She has made the weightless look heavy, the masculine seem feminine and vice versa, turning preconceived notions of appearances inside out or upside down. But in the planning of her house in East Hampton, Long Island, the artist's goal was to make a gracious, conducive setting for her art collection as well as space in which to live with and see her own work outside the studio environment. Unlike in a museum or a gallery, where the artificial lighting is fixed, Benglis wanted the opportunity to observe the natural changing light on her shiny reflective wall sculptures and massive cast bronzes,

Lynda Benglis

PREVIOUS PAGE: *Always experimenting with materials, Benglis had a sybaritic teak bath set into a redwood platform. The shower door and the sliding windows are sandblasted glass.* L E F T: *In this all-purpose room, stock sliding glass doors are installed at varying heights, one affording a view into the artist's double-height studio. Her 1985 glass sculptures balance on a gleaming granite and mahogany kitchen island; nearby are her 1968–71 bronze sculpture and a 1929 Mies van der Rohe lounge chair.* B E L O W: *At the great oak dining table, dinner often includes* Papadini, *a lentil pasta invented by molecular biologist Sarabhai. John Ahearn's 1984 sculpture hangs just below the point where bottom ceiling trusses stop short of the wall.*

and to create a situation that was accommodating but noncompetitive.

"It started as a very plain studio," says Benglis's architect, Louis Mannie Lionni. "Lynda was very clear about spatial needs and wanted a plain house with as few gratuitous gestures as possible." Decisions about siting and dimensions of the house were made quickly; selecting the right materials took longer.

Because the energy-efficient house is basically a large rectangle with a flat roof, Benglis felt an unconventional siding material was called for. Ultimately she and Lionni decided on Transite, a cement-based corrugated material that would complement the ribbon effect of the artist's fluted-column sculptures. The wavy surface would also create an unusual play of light and shadow when the sun filtered through the tall white pines that surround the house. The outdoor redwood decks were left unstained and have weathered to the same mellow gray as the siding.

A unique feature of the house, which is built into a hillside, is the way it interacts with its site. Outside the living room, a deck runs the length of the house. But on the other side of the room, where the hill falls away, the tops of pine trees are visible through sliding glass

doors raised a foot from the floor.

In landscaping, Benglis cut back the pine and oak forest, and in keeping with her exotic, unusual handling of materials, she planted voluminous plumed grasses, bamboo trees, and weeping dwarf pines to create a calm, contemplative atmosphere that contrasts with the vibrant art inside. Large boulders, near the house or on secluded terraces, are placed as carefully as her outdoor sculptures, and flat rocks serve as stepping stones along the winding paths.

The materials used throughout the interior were the result of many conversations between Benglis and Lionni about the feeling and integrity of the house. Among the few decorative elements are trusses made of wood and colored metal tubing that span the ceiling. Since the setting is private, the house was kept open to nature, with sliding window doors and skylights in almost every room. A variety of woods were used throughout the interior: All the trim is teak; the kitchen cabinets are a combination of stained mahogany and mahogany veneer that will weather differently; the ceilings are Douglas fir; the floors are yellow pine; and the stairs are oak. In the kitchen, slabs of sleek polished black granite are broken by two sequoia-red sinks.

Like the house, much of the art Benglis collects is minimal, such as the large canvas by Ron Gorchov or the muted pastel painting by Ralph Humphrey that hangs in the bedroom. Others, like a small female torso by John Ahearn, a work by Kenny Scharf, and many of Benglis's own pieces, fairly burst with energy. Every work has been given a generous amount of space, allowing each to stand out. Benglis's travels to India, where she has made cloth banners, and the influences of her companion, Anand Sarabhai, are evident in her house: The wood entrance doors were fabricated in India; Indian beds provide outdoor seating on the deck; and the couple's collection of Indian urns adds warmth to the otherwise high-tech simplicity.

It is an invigorating mix that reflects its occupants' active lifestyle. Lionni says about the success of the house, "It is so close to her own work as an artist and continues to be an evolving design process as well as a work in progress."

ABOVE: *Under the white pines, Benglis's 1975 fluted lead and aluminum sculptures, Primary Structures, are echoed by the pattern of the house's corrugated siding.*

LEFT: *In the bedroom, the artist's appreciation for archetypal shapes is reflected in her teaming of Rietveld's 1918 Red/Blue Chair and 1923 End Table, Ron Gorchov's 1974 shaped canvas, Walk, her own 1986 glass sculpture, and figures from New Guinea.*

spirited presence

The painter Nabil Nahas lives in TriBeCa, on a street that rumbles with passing trucks, but his loft has the quiet opulence of a grand apartment in Paris or Cairo. With its high ceilings, Oriental carpets, and gilt-and-velvet French Empire chairs (some covered in soft white cotton), it is, in many ways, a re-creation of the world Nahas knew as a child. ● Born in 1950 in Beirut, Lebanon, Nahas lived in Egypt until he was ten, when the family moved back to Beirut. Nahas acquired a knowledge of antiquities at an early age: He made his first visit to an archaeological site in Egypt when he was six years old. "At that time I was preoccupied with mummy cases," recalls Nahas, who would spend hours in the shop of an antiquities dealer, a family friend. "Once there was a big drama over my letter to Santa Claus because I asked for a sarcophagus, which

Nabil Nahas

PREVIOUS PAGE: *Wanting to "give the paintings a chance," Nahas covered his velvet upholstered French Empire furniture with loose cotton slipcovers. An Empire backgammon table holds Cazaux and Mayodon ceramics; at right, an Henri Michaux drawing.*
OPPOSITE: *French culture has always been important to Nahas; this small area boasts an Empire daybed, French café table, Chaim Soutine's* Still Life with Pike *on an easel, and a pencil drawing by Raoul Dufy below; behind, a 1982 Nahas canvas.*
BELOW: *The artist created separate seating areas in the open loft, defining them with special focal points such as Raoul Dufy's jardinière, Lenoble's turquoise ceramics on the dining table, or African laundry benches near the white-clad sofa. For further delineation, Nahas hangs one of his large acrylic-on-canvas paintings in each space, left to right, 1987, 1982, 1988.*
RIGHT: *The chaste lines of Jean-Michel Frank's limed oak cabinet and cane chairs are set in understated luxury. Alex Katz's cut-out* Ada *is behind the book- and object-laden table; in front, a 1809 Desmalater chair and T. H. Robsjohn-Gibbings stool.*

of course I never got." But the artist still has the amulets that he dug from sites on Byblos, and today his collection is scattered on the dining table in his art-packed loft.

Nahas grew up reading art books, which provided his first introduction to the New York School. "I knew about Pollock and Rothko from those books, but I didn't realize that by then most of them had died. And I had no idea how large the paintings were. It was purely on the basis of those books that I decided to come to New York." As it turned out, not until he had graduated from Yale was Nahas able to move to New York and begin his career as a painter in the proximity of museums housing great art.

Later, Nahas began collecting works by other artists, including Alex Katz, Henri Michaux, Joseph Santore, Chaim Soutine, Frank Moore, and Lucio Fontana. Setting off his collection is a discerning mix of furniture and objects that combines French gilt chairs and couches designed by Jacob Desmalter in 1809, a parchment screen by Jean-Michel Frank that forms a private corner for the cats and their bed, and African laundry benches. Nahas says he "stumbled across" his furniture, especially two pear-wood stools by T. H. Robsjohn-Gibbings wreathed

ABOVE: *The kitchen, with its pear-wood cabinetry, is an oasis of simplicity in the otherwise grand apartment. In front, works by Nahas and Nicholas Wilder hang over a fragment of a seventeenth-century French sculpture.*
RIGHT: *Nahas does extensive research on his collections and keeps his reference books in the bedroom. Works by Jacques Herold, Maurice Denis, and Raoul Dufy hang above the library desk lamp; at top center is Joseph Santore's 1988 canvas,* Irene; *just above the bed, a work by A.M.D. Patellière.* OPPOSITE: *Creating intriguing cultural and textural mixes is a hallmark of the artist; here he blends art by Calvin Churchman, Auguste Herbin, and Henri Michaux with a Russian*

provincial chair, a French canape, an African Senufo bench, and a Jean-Michel Frank parchment screen that hides the cats' bed.

with carved hounds. "They look like I could take them for a walk every morning," he jokes. That sense of humor is also apparent in the rare Raoul Dufy hand-painted ceramic jardinière that sits near equally precious books of Middle Eastern archaeological engravings.

"No matter how eclectic they might be, whether it is a chair or a vase, each object takes on a presence of its own," Nahas explains. "I think that it is the energy, the life that the artist, whatever craft he exercises, was able to embody or infuse into the object. The furniture is very pure, timeless, and in many ways, joins the aesthetic of the predynastic Egyptian objects. Whether I am aware of it or not, the colors and textures of the objects that I surround myself with seem to find their way into my paintings."

Nahas's large-scale paintings also hang in the loft. Against the pale gray-green walls, one majestic canvas of dark amorphous shapes in a field of gold seems to glow from within. "I would say it is like a spirit coming out," says Nahas, looking at the work. "Inhabited."

colorful vignettes

Housed in the skylit top floor of an old
warehouse in New York City's TriBeCa, the loft
shared by husband and wife painter Mel Bochner
and sculptor Lizbeth Marano serves as a vibrant
backdrop for the couple's constantly rotating exhibit
of artifacts, with blocks of saturated wall color
setting the tone. ● Truncated walls that stop short of
the pitched roofline define bedroom, living room,
and kitchen, and though most are painted pristine
white, various sections of both Sheetrock and brick
were transformed by color into what Bochner titles
his "Wall Paintings." On one such section, Bochner
painted a birthday present for Marano directly on a
wall, his characteristic flat geometric shapes seeming
to tumble through space. Another was painted an
intense pink, a color that was inspired by Mexican

Lizbeth Marano /
Mel Bochner

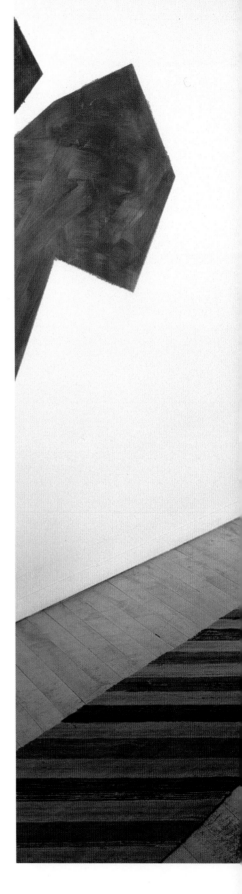

architect Luis Barragan and is heightened by the angle of the light from the bank of windows on the north side of the loft. The wall currently showcases a Brazilian Xingu headdress, an enormous circle of yellow, white, and dark brown feathers. In the kitchen, a glazed pot suggested the blue-green color of the brick wall, and more jolts of color are found in the niches put into the corridor leading to Marano's studio (Bochner's studio is at the entrance to the loft).

In this almost unbroken rectangular space, works of primitive art collected from around the world jut out from the expanses of intense, vivid wall color: objects that act as a springboard to extend the field of possibilities into new ideas, both in the artists' lives and in their art. "The things you see around you are tokens of our lives and our passion for art. They are in-spirational, and they are objects of great meaning in our life because they are integrated into our lives," says Bochner of their collection, which includes contemporary works by Eva Hesse, Sol Lewitt, Barry LeVa, and Elizabeth Murray, and artifacts from New Guinea, Mali, Africa, Italy, and more. Each color-bathed wall forms a self-contained tableau that demands a viewer study the object it offers

in a completely fresh way. Says Marano, "When we both decide we are no longer seeing what is on the wall, we change it. Then there is the fun of rediscovery to see them again. They've changed because you've changed."

Though observers of Bochner and Marano's extraordinary collection might disagree, they do not consider themselves collectors. The diverse objects "are like my ideas: I don't think I collected them as much as they collected me," says Bochner. "One of the interesting things about any collection is that individual pieces have one meaning, but in relationship to each other and to what the person does, they take on another meaning. The collections are also souvenirs of certain friendships with people who want to share their interest and fascination with primitive art, and of a particular time in our lives. Acquiring a work is also a kind of learning process, about other cultures and the quality of making something with a certain material. This gives dimension to one's life in the way a work is able to continue through the years. A balance that, for me, is a positive value."

ABOVE: *Another wall painting, this time executed by Marano for her daughter's bedroom, is based on Livia's Villa, a fresco housed in the Museo Nazionale Romano.*
RIGHT: *Faux mosaic tiles, made popular by the eighteenth-century discovery of Pompeii, are "a wonderful cross between the rococo and early Roman sensibilities," explains Bochner, who places the tiles on Marano's 1974 sideboard.*
OPPOSITE: *On the long, curved kitchen island, the couple displays a 1950s Madoura pitcher acquired on a visit to Vallauris.*

juxtaposing cultures

Bones, plants, fossils, ropes, and Renaissance, Greek, and Egyptian art are but a few of the sources that inspire Nancy Graves's eclectic paintings and sculptures. The artist is also fascinated by topography and contemporary technology, elements she uses to clarify or change perspective and scale in her work: whimsical overlappings of colored forms and historical references that Graves describes as "reverberations of the cycles of time."
● An early resident of Manhattan's SoHo, Graves lives in a loft that could be a deconstruction of any of her own works. Here, the disparate elements that comprise Graves's paintings and sculptures are reinforced by the art and objects that surround them: from the curves of a Queen Anne chair to the colors of an Alexander Calder mobile; from a haphazard tangle of bittersweet on a table to a thorn branch

Nancy Graves

repeated in a nearby painting, to orchids growing in an indoor garden. "I've never related specifically to those orchids, but I absorb them. The choice to include them in my loft as well as in my work, creates an affinity between the two," says Graves. She also sees a metaphor for her work in her collection of Indonesian shadow puppet sculptures. "They interest me for two reasons: for their delicacy and their physical strength, and also the way the positive and negative spaces were interfaced. Both these qualities are aspects of my work."

The shifting planes, odd juxtapositions, and borrowing of images that characterize Graves's work are also evident in the layout of her 10,000-square-foot loft and furniture groupings. A dramatic arch frames the entrance to a 2,500-square-foot gallery for her own paintings and sculptures; an almost blindingly white triangular kitchen with white marble countertops points toward the dining room. The long George III dining table surrounded by Queen Anne chairs in different styles holds twisted brass candle holders of contemporary design. Separating the area from the living room is a white folding screen that extends nearly the height and width of the loft.

The furniture in the living room

PREVIOUS PAGE: Graves often brings back objects from travels, which she then casts. These disparate elements are assembled into sculptures, integrated by both medium and means of color. TOP: The artist's interplay of cultural references is apparent in the kitchen, where a Tibetan monk's headdress, waist, and armband reside with figures from New Guinea and her 1982

bronze Visage. For the counters, Graves chose marble, "a material that relates to the beginnings of sculpture." ABOVE: In the gallery, a mahogany bench by Philippine national artist N. Veloso Abueva is displayed along with Graves's own recent works. OPPOSITE: Sinuous Queen Anne chairs in varying designs surround the long George III dining table.

ABOVE: *Illuminated bases give these Indonesian shadow puppets a modern twist. Behind, Graves's 1985–89* Cessnock *in oil, acrylic, and silver leaf on canvas with a propelling relief in anodized aluminum.* BELOW: *For her investigations into exotic cultures, the artist has assembled an impressive library. More artifacts and her watercolor* Curquenan, *1986, line the walls.* OPPOSITE: Ballarat, *1985, in oil, acrylic, and glitter with a painted aluminum extension, exemplifies Graves's varied palette and heavy surfaces; David Smith's 1951 sculpture balances on a pedestal of up-ended cinder blocks.*

epitomizes the ease with which Graves assembles contrasting shapes and textures; two upholstered Regency chairs trimmed in gold braid on black velvet are paired with an uncompromising 1830 Hudson River School bench and a low, intricate inlaid Chinese table. A David Smith painted steel sculpture rests on a pedestal of up-ended cinder blocks. Tucked in a corner near her studio is a library complete with stacks, rolling ladder, table, chairs, and pencils and paper for further research. More artifacts share the space.

Like her art, Graves's environment reflects her love of travel, her investigation and use of past and present cultures, "in an attempt to bring contemporary ways of thinking to these ageless images and icons." Though speaking of her work, Graves could have just as easily been describing her loft when she explains that with careful planning, execution, and development of space, "it is possible to start working in a particular direction and shift very rapidly with the juxtaposition of an additional element. This is incorporated into my overall intent."

tHE DWELLING AS A WORK OF

art is a better place . . . to live with,

and live for and by in every sense.''

Today's artists might well have

taken their cues from Frank Lloyd

Wright's 1957 pronouncement as

David Deutsch explores the possibilities of plywood in his upstate New York home.

they push their personal aesthetics beyond the studio and into

their homes: a balancing act of exploring materials for practical

The Home as

purposes while imposing their artistic styles. Whether these

projects for specific sites are a re-creation or a further realization

of ideas, the artists' entire world becomes a canvas, so to speak, one that diminishes, even obscures, the delicate line between fine and applied art, where not even the smallest detail such as a doorknob or switch plate is immune to scrutiny. The artist-turned-architect-furniture-maker strives to leave a mark of individuality to such an extent that the home becomes a testing ground, a place for working through experimental concepts that later may reappear in a painting. It is this nonstop interweaving of ideas that transforms a home into a work of art. Each artist

Work of Art

makes this transformation a unique statement. Californians Billy Al Bengston and Charles Arnoldi disdain almost anything ready-made, as it doesn't suit their innate aesthetic. Bengston explains,

"Most furniture and architecture is made out of convenience. And oftentimes, when things are prefabricated, they don't fit your real life. Almost everything we live with nowadays is part of a plan made to fit someone we don't know."

Specimen evergreens and rare trees surround the pool.

The entrance to Ossorio's studio.

And Bengston, frustrated by schemes "made out of the size of the ruler and the size of the module," makes the most of his insouciant furniture by hand. Charles Arnoldi explores the relationships of bold materials mixed with the ordinary, another expression of the artist still rooted in a fine-art mode. Izhar Patkin, in his offbeat, nonchalant style, turned a floor of a factory on New York's Lower East Side into a concoction of ethnic sensibilities. In TriBeCa, Arman expresses his love of music by fusing parts of musical instruments

Treasures crowd an intimate sitting room on the East Hampton estate of Edward Dragon and the late Alfonso Ossorio y Yangco.

into the forms of his idiosyncratic furniture. And David Deutsch turned the inside of his upstate New York concrete-block complex into a Usonian extravaganza of plywood.

Shell-encrusted objets in one of the estate's baths.

These artists are energized by a stronger, more deliberate alliance with their living quarters, which in turn offer implicit definitions of their occupants.

Most of it is just like painting," muses Billy Al Bengston of his house in Venice, a spacious structure that is as much a studio, a playhouse, a gallery, and even a garage (Bengston is a motorcycle enthusiast, among other things) as it is a home. Change is what this artist is all about, and not surprisingly since Bengston's art has also shifted from early chevron work to recent canvases exploring the dynamics of colorful grids. "The grid, lines intersecting one another, is an old method of dividing space. It is a point of focus," he says. And those multidirectional focal points keep the work flowing and the environment in a state of flux.

One day he might overhaul the plumbing or electricity, another might find him moving walls or thinking about enlarging his vegetable garden. "When you get your house perfect, you should either

Billy Al Bengston

PREVIOUS PAGE: *Bengston painted the poured concrete floors in the entrance foyer using a mop and squeegee to push around the acrylic paint (the same brand he employs in his paintings). The soft, burnished colors offset the jagged edges of the artist's hardwood and Formica table and the intense pigments of his 1969 painting,* Sonora Dracula. *The artist's* Key Largo *faces the living room, where another 1990 acrylic on canvas work,* Nesibanebtet, *hangs.* LEFT, TOP TO BOTTOM: *In an upstairs bath, Bengston applied marble moldings with fractured edges over a startling jolt of red on the acrylic-painted floor. A Balinese wooden palm mimics the outdoor landscape. A bath doubles as a greenhouse.* RIGHT AND OPPOSITE: *After the carpeting was laid, Bengston inserted shapes cut from rug samples, then added lines drawn on with a felt-tip marker.* Blue Cavern Draculas, 1976, *is from a series of acrylic paintings on canvas fabricated into a screen. An irregular-shaped Bengston-made desk in hardwoods and Formica stands before a door leading to the pool; at left,* Tunduma, 1988.

demolish it or move,'' Bengston quips. When he is not working on the house (which he shares with his wife, Christi, their daughter, Blue T.I.C.A., and three Manchester terriers), or running, swimming, or cooking, he is painting, either at his Hawaiian outpost or here in California. The ease of air travel makes the homes interchangeable. ''Each locale affects what I'm going to paint. It's just a dinner in the air between places.''

Wall space that is not taken by Bengston's own paintings is devoted to works by a close-knit group of fellow Californians including Ed Moses, Laddie John Dill, Ron Davis, Charles Arnoldi, and Ed Ruscha.

covered the seats and backs of its chairs (the generic office variety) in pink, blue, and yellow neon plush. Even Bengston's floors, ranging from poured concrete to Douglas fir to oak, and doors and windows in various shapes and sizes (which he designed) reflect his playful aesthetic. "I'd like to design everything," says Bengston quite seriously. "It would be more convenient."

The landscaping around the house is no more immune to Bengston's experimentation than its interior. Flanking a seventy-five-foot lap pool are separate garden areas: one for cacti, another for vegetables and fruit, a goldfish pond with water lillies and tropical plants; an improvised hothouse for orchids is in a bath. The Bengstons needn't travel far for fresh produce. They can pick lemons, limes, and avocados from the trees; herbs, lettuce, tomatoes, and berries from the vegetable plot. Wild parrots, lizards, and a rope hammock strung between two King palms make this home even more paradisiacal. The artist says, "Lettuce grows in two weeks. If you add spaghetti with the basil that grows all year long, how can you go wrong? Life is good here. And it gets better all the time as long as you don't do too many stupid things. You just have to improve it."

There is sculpture, too: bronze figures by Robert Graham, ceramic works by Kenneth Price and Peter Voulkos, and a sculpture by DeWain Valentine.

Bengston has designed inlaid cabinets, rugs, chairs, and tables cut into simple, often quirky shapes and has infused his ideas with the same sly humor and whimsy that characterize his personality. A carved terrier leaps through the base of the dining room table, and Bengston

ABOVE: *Spike basks beside the lap pool, aluminum teahouse, and herb and vegetable gardens. At the west end are the artist's indoor and outdoor painting studios.* RIGHT: *Another view of the living room from under the teahouse canopy.* OPPOSITE: *In his landscaping details, just as in his work, Bengston incorporates grids in vibrating primary colors, framing areas in wood, wire, and tile.*

plywood mania

David Deutsch's country house is just a short drive from Olana, the grand, eccentric Moorish-style home where Frederic Edwin Church lived and painted his Hudson River Valley landscapes, but the parallels between the two artists are only geographic; Deutsch's house is as resolutely plain as Church's was ornate. Nor are Deutsch's panoramic canvases inspired by the 190 acres of farmland and woods that surround his complex of buildings. "They're from my preconceived ideas," says Deutsch, whose paintings in cool spectrums of color are of a "mechanical, internalized nature." • Deutsch bought his property in 1984 and designed the main house, guest house, and studio himself. "The concept was to make a minimal formal garden with buildings acting as cornerstones: These buildings are, in a sense, volumes or cubes, all more or less

David Deutsch

PREVIOUS PAGE:
Deutsch conceived his "easy-to-make" furniture of squares in various sizes; where the grains intersect, the plywood appears to be in different colors. In the corridor between the living and dining areas, a hardwood cabinet was stained to resemble ebony; at the end, a Patrick Hogan work.

equal," says the artist. "The house is divided into two buildings with a connecting hallway: two cubes. The bedroom with a bathroom is equal to a living room with a kitchen and dining area. The studio is a big cube. And they were made with the intention of slowly developing a network."

In realizing his scheme, Deutsch utilized inexpensive, common building materials such as glass, concrete blocks, and plywood, and like the Usonian houses of Frank Lloyd Wright, he set his one-story structures close to the ground on a site that was sheltered by a grove of white pines. "I wanted the house to assimilate and sit comfortably on the site without destroying the natural lay of the land," says Deutsch.

The interior walls, ceilings, cabinets, and rolling storage cart in the main house are fashioned entirely of plywood. In fact, Deutsch's use of plywood is so ubiquitous, the rooms resemble the inside of a giant plywood sculpture. Lighting, cleverly hidden under plywood baffles on the ceiling, changes the color of the plywood walls, making the rooms glow. Deutsch designed the linear dining room table and chairs as well as the couches and ottomans in the living area, also of plywood, and even had the upholstery fabric custom

OPPOSITE, ABOVE: *Like an efficient restaurant's, Deutsch's kitchen boasts stainless-steel surfaces, plus convenient plywood open shelving and a rolling cart. A mosaic of one-inch tiles covers the countertops.* OPPOSITE, BELOW: *Deutsch carried the plywood theme right down to the last nuance, commissioning the faux-wood textiles that cover his furniture in the living room. The space is highlighted by William Wegman's 1986 painting and Steve Keister's suspended 1985 sculpture.* LEFT: *Cabinetmaker-artist Steven Piscuskas's executions of Deutsch's furniture designs were proportioned to specific sites in each cubic building; in the dining room the double-sided fireplace's steel screen can slide up into the chimney wall.*

LEFT: *Deutsch's* **Standing Library Desk** *with lounge chair webbing and folding aluminum tubular sides makes reference to outdoor living. The 1989 desk was commissioned by A/D, New York. Faceted pyramid building blocks usually found on exteriors were used to face the fireplace wall. A Diana Donaldson photograph hangs over a Deutsch-designed bookshelf.*

ABOVE: *The buildings of Deutsch's complex nestle comfortably into the landscape; the artist is training vines over the exterior concrete blocks to make them even less obtrusive.*

woven to simulate the look and texture of plywood. The only departures are the sliding glass doors and the burst of color provided by blue, green, and gold Italian glass tiles, which cover the kitchen and bath counters, completely line the tub and shower, make up a sunken fountain in the garden, and define the edge of the swimming pool.

Living in an artwork is second nature to Deutsch, who grew up in Los Angeles. "All the California artists I know designed their own homes and studios. It was absolutely consistent with their feelings about aesthetic space. In New York, you got a loft, threw a bed in it, a hot plate, maybe a shower. You thought more about the work, and you lived in the dust of the work. In L.A. you lived *in* the work. That was the big difference."

Always a perfectionist, Deutsch concedes the limitations of such a circumscribed design scheme. "If I were to go on and design a second house, I would probably be a little more generous with materials and living space," he admits. And yet, Deutsch would still be pursuing his utopian dream using the same common materials elevated to grandeur through brilliant design.

ABOVE: *Deutsch's master plan to construct "a network of buildings with straight lines of hedges between them" included a separate guest house. This ingenious one-room dwelling has its own fireplace and a rolling banquette that becomes a full-size bed. Only a Richard Artschwager–designed table set on a Chinese rug and a Corbusier chair diverge from the plywood theme.* RIGHT: *The artist's cubic studio building.* OPPOSITE: *Frank Lloyd Wright originated the utilitarian one-material tenet that Deutsch addresses throughout his complex.*

Here again the artist uses one-inch tiles and, from the face of his bedroom fireplace wall to the perimeter of the bathtub, the pyramid block motif.

world color

Before he moved to the United States, Izhar Patkin lived on a kibbutz in his native Israel. Like the other members, he had his own stone house, but it wasn't big enough for Patkin. "I was always a space hog," admits the artist, who decided to extend his living quarters with a tent he purchased from a tribe of nomadic Bedouins living nearby. "It became an integral part of the house because I put carpets outside, and it looked as though the house was just the entrance, and the tent was the living room. The neighbors thought I was eccentric, but I took it very seriously: I had more space." ● Since moving to New York in 1979, Patkin has applied that same iconoclasm and improvisation to his art and later to his Lower East Side loft. In his early paintings, Patkin, who studied at the Corcoran and later attended the Whitney Independent Study Program,

Izhar Patkin

PREVIOUS PAGE: *Partially concealed by a Robert Kushner painting, Patkin installed a glass-paneled entrance door made for a suburban house between his studio and living area. A 1985 Patkin painting hangs above an Elsa Rady porcelain installation; Kim MacConnel is represented by a collage and his painted chair; two works of Nam June Paik are below another work by Patkin.* RIGHT: *To heighten "a kind of Third World context" in the already vivacious scene, the artist places his silver-leaf-on-wood* Dolcinea *and anodized aluminum* Don Quijote *in front of a wall* packed edge to edge with works of art. ABOVE: *McDermott and McGough's photograph hangs above the laundry room entrance.* OPPOSITE: *A "flower power" theme painted by Joseph Horatio engulfs the tiny kitchen.*

used such unconventional materials as rubber sheets, anodized aluminum, window screens, and wax. A recent series, "The Five Senses," is composed of five paintings, each one representing Patkin's interpretation of a sense. "The eyes are Buddha eyes, a little Oriental," Patkin says. "The ear has a big Indian-style earring. The mouth is from a bearded Georgian."

Like his work, Patkin's neighborhood is a mixture of ethnic diversity, with brightly colored Puerto Rican storefronts, Italian bakeries, street vendors, kosher delis. Even the smells collide and mingle, and wafting from windows or blasting from cars, the strains of a mazurka mix with heavy metal rock. All are a preparation for what is to come inside the artist's studio-home.

His loft has undergone much the same transformation as his home on the kibbutz. A former dog collar factory that had been abandoned for years, its windows were boarded up, the floors were littered with rhinestones and old bills, and the walls were decorated with posters of poodles. "It was a magical wreck," recalls Patkin.

Without actually altering the layout of his loft, Patkin managed to change its character entirely. He began by

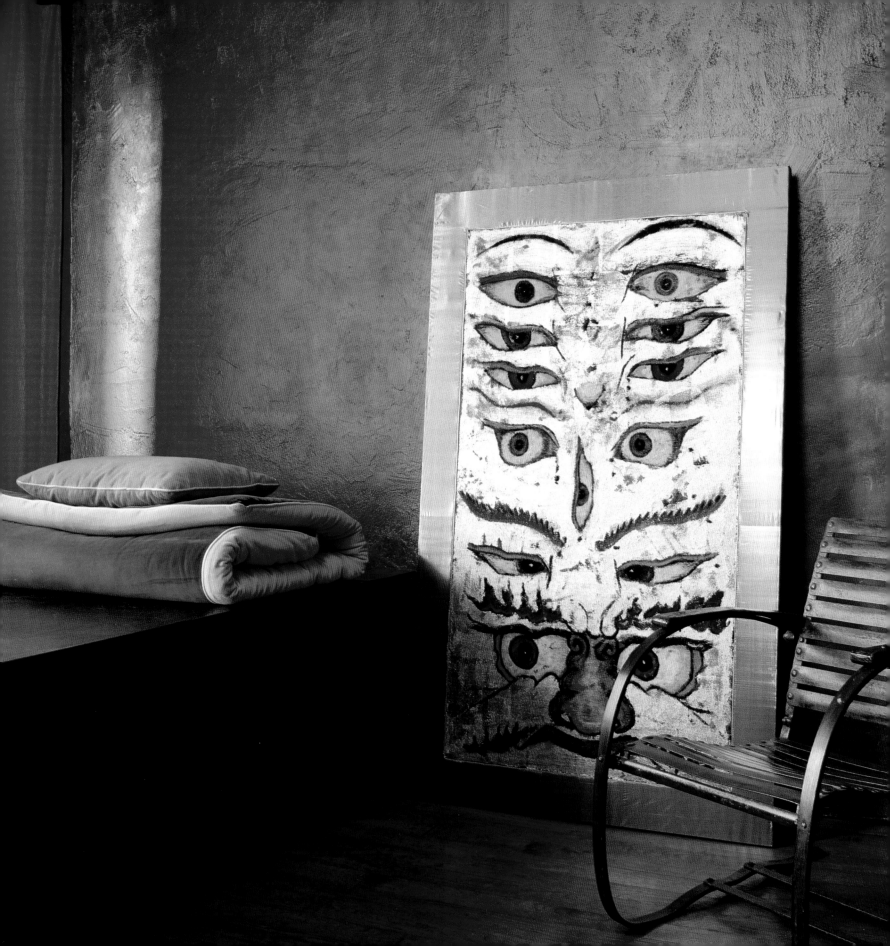

making five columns out of Sheetrock
to create the main room, covering
the floor with an enormous canvas
painted to resemble old linoleum and
then stenciled with clusters of
flowers. A friend who worked at a
nightclub painted the tiny kitchen in
hallucinatory-bright colors. Patkin
painted the top half of the cellophane-
draped front ''adjunct'' room walls
in a cool white; the bottom half is
Caribbean blue, the two halves
separated by an orange stripe topped
with a stenciled row of chickens.
Lastly, a suburban-type front door was
inserted to separate his studio from
the rest of the loft and to keep out the
turpentine fumes.

Still mindful of his childhood and
fascinated by the ways of his adopted
country, Patkin says, ''Where I grew
up, it is common to live in a house
that is two thousand years old, where
making a change was always a big
commitment. Then I came to this
country and discovered a Sheetrock
mentality. You can just take a mat
knife and move a door from one side
of a room to another because you need
room for a painting or because you are
sick of it. Put a wall up, take a wall
down. It's no big deal. The house
is really like throwing a tent up.''

ABOVE: *Patkin
adorned a flea-market
lamp with dangling
Greek, Mexican, and
Indian souvenirs; its
pierced shade casts
eerie shadows on Nam
June Paik's* Robot.
*Paused on the screen is
a clip from a video
collaboration with
Paik.* RIGHT:
*Patkin's patterned
rubber curtains
provide the backdrop
for a painted wrought-
iron chair.* OPPOSITE:
*Patkin does a complete
turnaround in a
meditative, spartan
second bedroom,
where he can observe
his 1991 painting from
"The Five Senses"
series and a small
Nikki Moser work.*

With bold strokes and equally bold materials, Charles Arnoldi has pushed his artistic vision beyond the boundaries of the studio, creating a home that is, in every respect, a further realization of his art. "Your environment becomes part of your work because you are making art everyday, wherever you go. So it starts to accumulate a look of what you like and what you dislike. You can tell a lot about a person by looking at his or her environment. It's as dangerous as telling someone your dreams." ● Using materials in unexpected ways always appealed to the artist, who began his art career in the late 1960s building constructions of tree branches. Later, he would explore the same theme using twigs and branches as models for cast and assembled bronze sculptures that he fabricates in his own foundry. By the eighties, Arnoldi had started his "chainsaw"

Charles Arnoldi

works in layers of laminated plywood, hacked with a chainsaw to produce a synthesis of slashes, then painted over with radiant colors.

Recent works, however, have been executed in more traditional media, such as oil on canvas and cast bronze. "I've been trying to turn my enthusiasm away from materials, as they figure too heavily into the way the pieces are interpreted," says the artist. "What I want to do is force myself off-track for a while. It's an exercise in discipline."

Instead, Arnoldi has redirected his passion for texture and materials into his new house, a rectangular concrete structure overlooking the Pacific in Malibu, where he and his wife, Katie, and their son and daughter spend weekends and summers. "The idea was to build a big box, very much like a lot of studios I've lived in in the past. You find some square footage, a shell. You move in, and you make do with whatever you have; you can

PREVIOUS PAGE:
"I've always worked in different directions at once," says the artist, whose stucco-faced oceanfront house gives evidence of a foray into architecture. LEFT:
Accented by Thonet chairs, Arnoldi fashioned the plywood table in proportion to the dining area. Above, a square ash-framed window revolves on center pins when gently pushed.

ABOVE: *One of Arnoldi's most intricate concepts is this pivoting door, which contains a glass panel of laser-cut drawings laminated between two pieces of sandblasted glass. The glass is welded into square aluminum sand-finished frames. At right, his 1990 monoprint.* LEFT: *Arnoldi designed most of his furniture, including the leather sofas, chairs, and ottoman, steel tables, and carpets that are reinterpretations of his tree-branch paintings; atop Isamu Noguchi's 1944 ovoid table is a Frank Gehry sculpture. Behind, the artist's 1990* Crowded Vacuum *in acrylic, modeling paste, sticks, sawed logs, and branches on plywood. Through the second-story opening is Lynda Benglis's 1972* Knot; *in the niche below, a Frank Gehry maquette for an edition of cardboard chairs.*

LEFT: *Stairwells become sculptural forms encompassing a range of common building materials. Top to bottom: Four-by-four steel tubing painted with a dull red rust-preventive primer supports the solid ash stairs leading to his studio. Rejoined ash plywood becomes a sliding door outside the master suite; the ladder accessing the skylight above is solid ash four-by-fours. Coarse-grained oak plywood repeats the zigzag pattern of the black rubber steps.*
RIGHT: *Matte-finished white Formica cabinets form an unbroken line in the kitchen; Arnoldi used a marble wall between the finely polished granite slabs, which are also installed on the counters and the backsplashes. On the dining table is the artist's 1988* Oddball, No. 1, *of cast and assembled bronze with dry pigment and patina.*

modify it later. And that is exactly what I have created."

Although Arnoldi is still experimenting with new possibilities, the house is already a symbol of his perfectionism. His fascination with using materials in unorthodox ways is apparent throughout, and not just in the furniture he has designed, such as a plywood dining table, a capacious leather couch and chairs, and steel tables for the living room. A door is not just a door in Arnoldi's home: It's sandblasted glass panels in aluminum frames, or solid sanded aluminum sheets, or laminated plywood with diagonally cut lozenges.

But the most striking aspect of this

LEFT: *Arnoldi experimented with the possibilities of cement, adding colored pigment to the floors of the master bath to contrast with the rough texture of the steel-trowled cement walls.*
ABOVE AND RIGHT: *To soften the hard-edged appearance of the dramatic architecture, Arnoldi laid pale wall-to-wall* *carpeting the color of a breaking wave in the master bedroom; a Frank Gehry carving is in the niche between the windows facing the sea.* TOP RIGHT: *The artist had aluminum sanded and brushed on the sliding pocket door in another part of the bath; the result, a machined finish with a hand-made appeal.*

house is its epic proportions. Most of the ground-floor ceilings are twenty feet high; in the living room, sliding glass doors that look out over the ocean are a massive fifteen feet high and twenty-five feet wide. So far, though, Arnoldi has not allowed himself time to enjoy the view. "If it is daylight, I can't sit down to save my soul. But I am trying to appreciate the luxury of the house, and learn to take the time to sit, think, and read books."

ABOVE: *On the ocean side of the house, Arnoldi continues his explorations of cast concrete, devising a circular table and benches, the complement to a matching square set.*
RIGHT: *Against the backdrop of another tinted stucco wall, rare cacti in artist-designed concrete forms line the approach to the house.*

collecting, amassing, accumulating

By the time Arman moved to New York in 1963, he had long since established himself in France with his daring "Accumulations," sculptures and painted assemblages that fused dozens of similar man-made objects, including violins, swords, paint scrapers, and brushes. A leading *nouveau réaliste*, Arman saw a treasure trove of possibilities on the streets of New York City. "When I first came to New York, I did not intend to stay, but I fell in love with the city because it was a paradise of accumulation," says the artist, who was captivated by his first walk along Canal Street. "Ready-mades of accumulations: job lotters and everything." ● On the top floor of a four-story building in TriBeCa, a former pickle factory with a clear view of the Hudson River and beyond, Arman, his wife, Corice, and their children are surrounded by objects; like his assemblages, the

Arman

Afghanistan chair and French Art Nouveau vase.

LEFT AND OPPOSITE: *The artist originally collected fetish African art as a counterpoint to his own work. Here, the fierceness of the nail-studded Congo figures and a standing nineteenth-century artifact from the Agiba tribe (used to display ancestors' skeletons) is subdued by the geometric lines of Art Deco furniture and a Frank Stella painting from his "Concentric Squares" series.* BELOW: *Arman's idiosyncratic musical chairs are surprisingly comfortable; behind, a Jean Michel Basquiat oil and a Tiffany lamp.*

PREVIOUS PAGE: *Arman often repeats themes in different mediums. From his 1961 painting, NBC Rage, come the fractured string instrument parts that are woven into the carpet. Seventeenth- and eighteenth-century Yoroï Japanese armor flanks the entry gallery, at ease with an*

groups are displayed as works of art. Arman admits he enjoys the competition between his art and his environment. "One thinks about three categories: collecting, amassing, and accumulating, which are translated in my work. It is a pack-rat instinct that is embedded in my mind, and I use it in my work as I use it in my home. Even with some of the works that I collect, I have a tendency to rebuild; to put them in a pattern of accumulation."

A prelude of what is to come is established the moment one enters the living quarters: Two full suits of traditional seventeenth- and eighteenth-century Japanese samurai armor greet visitors with their fearsome intricate beauty, and more headpieces fill the hallway shelves. One of the world's largest groups of brass Bakota sculptures from Gabon hold court in the dining room, and Arman's third-floor office is home to his collections of colorful Bakelite and Fenolite radios, crammed edge to edge on shelves. All are objects of function, past and present. Throughout, Arman juxtaposes his collections with tables, chairs, and place settings of his own design.

Arman becomes an expert on his objects, he feels, the curator of his own museum. "Choice is an

ABOVE: *The artist modeled the cast legs of the twin dining tables on the double bass; his candelabra adorn the marble tops. A collection of Bakota sculptures, the most important examples placed in front, create an accumulation of their own. Samurai head gear lines the top of the English Regency sideboard with Arman's 1957* Mauve Administratif, *above.* RIGHT: *Whether an assemblage of bulbs in Arman's 1959 light fixture or boxes of nails in* Petite Quincaillerie, *1964, the mass makes the single object difficult to identify. Alongside Tadaki· Kawayama's 1985 screen is Yves Klein's 1961* Venus.

OPPOSITE: *Arman's* Frozen Civilization, *a 1971* poubelle *steel work immersed in Plexiglas, and* Les Mousquetaires, *1962, correlate to two works of Pop art, Roy Lichtenstein's 1963 drawing and George Segal's* Portrait of Corice, *1974. The artist-designed low table with cast instrument legs holds a Bernar Venet bronze; Richard Stankiewicz's wall relief is in the four-story glass-enclosed atrium.*

important thing. When I collect something, I read books, I go to see collections, I go to museums. I look at the object and see different levels of quality: quality as an antique piece, and quality as a work of art, which means for me that the work was made by a good artist. I have criteria of quality for objects that are manufactured, too, like radios—the color, the design, and the rarity of some of them. I am always trying to get the top in quality as well as in rarity. Very ambitious."

The prolific collector is also a prolific artist, and he uses the same discrimination in his choices of materials. "Artists are always witnessing something. Every time we have a storm in New York, you see a lot of broken umbrellas lying in the streets. I have seen those umbrellas for thirty years, and I have been tempted to pick them up in a truck and make a mural out of them. I'm tempted, but I still haven't done it. One day I might. I'm sure you can gather one hundred umbrellas in two hours on the streets of New York." Meanwhile, the self-professed "born again" painter continues each of his series of accumulations, "faithful to my unfaithfulness."

A renovated barn serves as Al Held's open living quarters.

j

JASPER JOHNS SAYS HIS FLAG paintings came to him in a dream, and it is from the wellsprings of imagination, elusive and capricious, that inspiration is called forth. Artists, whose lives and work depend on inspiration, know this all too well, and become expert at shaping environments that stimulate creative thinking.

The Home as

Their homes offer clues, even direct evidence, to the kinds of work they produce. For Jan Hashey, who draws household objects, inspiration abounds in her Catskill home. There, her collection of brown bowls serves as the model for her precise work. Ed Baynard's collection of pottery and flower gardens has provided him with ideas for subject matter for his classically composed watercolor still lifes. The disparate shapes of his collection of art pottery and their placement in his home continue to remind him of "the rightness of order," a ruling principle in his work. Some artists are inspired by the energy of an abundance of collectibles. Tavlos has filled his colorful Santa Fe

Inspiration

adobe house with kitschy bric-a-brac from flea markets, Native American handicrafts, plants, and anything else that catches his fancy, and elements of all of these "finds" wend their way into his bright, graphic paintings. New Mexico is also home to the minimalist painter Agnes Martin, but her adobe home is as rigorously pared down as her sublimely re-

Connecticut resident Ilse Getz creates a colorful framed collage with favorite pieces of jewelry.

ductive canvases. For Martin, inspiration comes from within,

Pre-Bismarck German measuring instruments hang in George Rickey's New York State compound.

stirred only by the vastness of the not-quite desert and the sounds of a Beethoven symphony. Californian Peter Alexander is aroused by light, his Marina del Rey home arranged for total relaxation among the props he has orchestrated for pure, unfettered daydreaming. In New York, realist painter Richard Estes's paints, work tools, and photographic equipment are arranged as carefully as the elements in one of his hyper-realistic paintings; perfection is a way of life in his home as well as in his work. Each

A Catskill Mountain view from the deck of Al Held's home.

of these homes, whether carefully ordered or a riotous jumble of objects and color, seems to be ripe with possibilities, a place where the unexpected happy accidents that trigger inspiration are not just allowed but

One of a multitude of collections in Robert Cottingham's 1758 Connecticut farmhouse.

invited. For inspiration, to paraphrase the words of kinetic sculptor George Rickey, is chance, the sly muse who comes uninvited but is always ready to touch the artist with her wing.

room service

At certain times of the year, sunlight refracts off an odd-shaped piece of coated glass propped against the wall in Peter Alexander's apartment, sending a beam of light skimming along the gray carpet like an electrical charge. Alexander cherishes such serendipitous moments, for they spark the artist's imagination, inspiring his aerial perspective paintings of a world charged by its vivid natural occurrences. ● Alexander's space is kept resolutely minimal to provide an empty but skillfully lit stage for these natural flights of fancy. Iridescent dots of light, cast by the mirrored ballroom sphere hanging in the center of the artist's large open apartment, dance like constellations on the ceiling. "Light," says the native Angeleno, "is the key thread. Of all of our perceptions, light arouses the greatest desire. It suggests something ethereal, something

Peter Alexander

that is magical and otherworldly.''

Alexander likes to think of his living quarters in this concrete industrial building as a large hotel room: a place with little to distract him from daydreaming. ''My daughter describes the whole room as neo L.A. Zen, meaning lean, I suppose,'' says Alexander. Like a hotel room, it has matching double beds which face an imposing television. Singular objects with no particular purpose sit casually on the floor: a heavy bright blue ball, a deep-red velvet crate.

A map of the world takes up most of one wall. The intense Southern California light, filtered through semidrawn blinds, gives the room a calm, mysterious glow and sets the atmosphere for imagining and pictorializing far-off places and making them present. ''I see Morocco on the map. Then I think about Bergman and Bogart in *Casablanca*. It kicks off such indelible fantasies that are felt with such strength,'' says Alexander. ''I say to myself, 'How can I make paintings like that . . . that will kick off that stuff and release the mind to never-never land?' ''

PREVIOUS PAGE AND ABOVE: *An eight-by-eight-foot plywood table, designed by Alexander for the living area, doubles as his library.* BELOW: *Open shelves in the kitchen reflect the artist's quest for convenience (the gourmet food shop is just down the block). Above them hangs his* fiery 1991 Burbank. OPPOSITE: *Alexander's pared-down sleeping alcove features his 1974 painting on velvet,* The Other One.

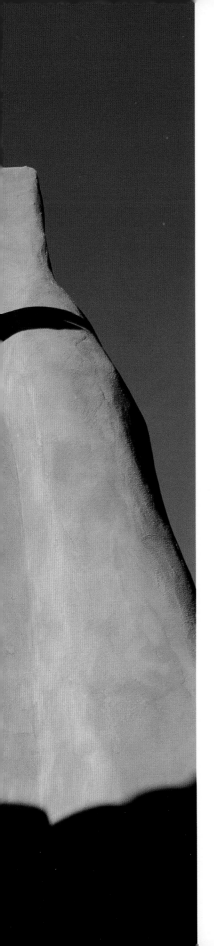

Santa Fe is an arid town in the Tesuque Valley where half of the population is descended from the Spanish settlers who came to the region four hundred years ago. Pueblo Indians, speaking their own language and English, mix with the Spanish-speaking population. So when Tavlos, a first-generation Greek-American raised in Illinois, moved to Santa Fe in 1970, he immediately felt at home with the foreignness of its sights and sounds. "It was obvious that this was not America, and yet it was in America," recalls Tavlos, who had traveled to Greece as a child. "I could be in Greece right now. The ocean is missing, and that is it. Otherwise, the vigas, the adobe construction, and the color are all Greece to me." ● Tavlos's fascination with the grandeur of the desert, the light, the mountains, and the Hispanic and Indian cultures quickly took root in

Tavlos

PREVIOUS PAGE: *The passive solar gain adobe house in chiaroscuro against a winter sky.* RIGHT: *Under broad vigas and cedar latillas, the interior of the house is a cacophony of color, from the ubiquitous neckerchiefed Sonny Boy to the reclining thirties plaster Indian the artist found at a local flea market. Rugs of Greek, Turkish, Navajo, and Egyptian origin mingle with one that translates the artist's bold work into textile form.* OPPOSITE, TOP AND BOTTOM: *Scarcely a surface in the artist's home escapes his razor-sharp graphics. Painted cut-outs pattern cabinet doors and frame the mirror in the bath and create a welcoming entrance.* OPPOSITE, CENTER: *Another kachina doll from Tavlos's collection.*

his art. He rented a house on a large ranch just outside of Santa Fe and started to paint. Six years later, he paid a call on his neighbor, Joseph Bakos, one of the original *Cinco Pintores* who had homesteaded twelve hundred acres when the land was still isolated piñon country. In exchange for paintings and a little cash, Tavlos acquired a piece of property. "It was an incredible gift from one artist to another," he says. With skills he had learned in architecture classes and with help from a neighbor, a fraternity brother, Tavlos built his two-story adobe home in six months, imbedding pot shards and mystical symbols in the corners of the house for good luck. His second-floor studio overlooks the double-height dining room. Today, the artist and his wife, Pamela Preston, share their home, "The Resurrection Studio," with their two dogs, Ouzo and Luna, their cat, P-cone, and a canary, Elvis-Pepe.

The architecture of the house is as sensuous as the distant Dos Titos mountains; its hand-molded adobe walls are curved and contoured into a play of forms reminiscent of the graphic patterns in Tavlos's art. Inside, the walls are a kaleidoscope of high-key colors in hot pinks, saturated purples, and brilliant blues that

complement the outrageous palette of his hard-edged paintings and sculpture. Yet the rooms are airy, each with its own cozy character. From the hand-picked local woods that make up the latillas and broad vigas on the ceiling to the nooks and crannies that are dug out of the walls, there is a feeling of oneness with the landscape.

The zany mix-up of cultures and art gives the interior the feeling of a miniature folk art museum, with curious kachina dolls; Tavlos's colorful zigzag designs on mirrors, doors, and rugs; flea market "finds"; and Navajo, Hopi, and Egyptian weavings competing for attention with Tavlos's whimsical art.

The howling coyote, nicknamed Sonny Boy, is one of Tavlos's best-known images. A symbol of the spiritual messenger in Indian lore, the image is used as a vehicle to express both pain and grief or great joy. The artist says, "When you come across the coyotes in winter, they look like they just came out of the dry cleaner, so clean, so beautiful. Almost every night you can hear the coyotes. When they come out and you hear them wail, it sounds like there are a million coyotes singing right outside your door. The message is there for each to interpret in his or her own way."

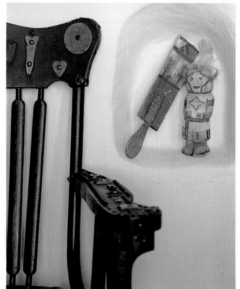

ABOVE AND RIGHT: *Tavlos tiled a portrait of Saint Pasquale, patron of the kitchen, into the alcove enclosing the stove; more tiles and carved wooden masks frame the alcove.* **LEFT:** *Behind a folk-art rocker, an antique kachina doll and an Indian artifact are propped in a small cranny dug out of the bedroom wall.*

LEFT: *Shelves framing the entrance to the dining area resemble a well-laden toymaker's shop filled with "finds" and art.*
ABOVE: *Tavlos's vibrant palette has touched even the entrance to the house.*
RIGHT: *Adobe can easily be coaxed and contoured by hand into an endless variety of* shapes, *like the step-patterned low wall that continues the flow of space between rooms.*
BELOW: *Steps flanking the chimney of the Kiva fireplace display objects in this sitting room, with the logs stacked in tepee fashion.*

picture perfect

Like Ralph Goings, Robert Cottingham, and other realist painters who came to prominence in the late 1960s and based their work on photographs, Richard Estes was tagged a photo-realist for his fastidiously rendered cityscapes. But Estes was never truly comfortable with the photo-realist label. "I am a realist," says Estes firmly, "and I use photographs just as Thomas Eakins used photographs. The camera is basically a kind of sketchbook, so I take around five hundred pictures at one time. It sounds like a lot, but I can do it in an afternoon, just clicking away. If I am going to spend three months on a work, I don't want to be stingy with references." ● For Estes, living and working in the city presents a welcome challenge. "In a way," he explains, "I'm trying to organize chaos. When something is organized, it's at rest. It's peaceful, even though there

Richard Estes

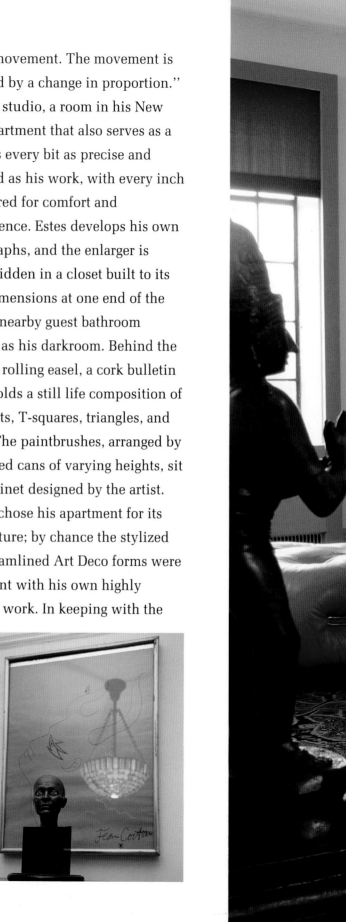

can be movement. The movement is balanced by a change in proportion." And his studio, a room in his New York apartment that also serves as a study, is every bit as precise and balanced as his work, with every inch engineered for comfort and convenience. Estes develops his own photographs, and the enlarger is neatly hidden in a closet built to its exact dimensions at one end of the room; a nearby guest bathroom doubles as his darkroom. Behind the massive rolling easel, a cork bulletin board holds a still life composition of snapshots, T-squares, triangles, and rulers. The paintbrushes, arranged by size in red cans of varying heights, sit on a cabinet designed by the artist.

Estes chose his apartment for its architecture; by chance the stylized and streamlined Art Deco forms were consistent with his own highly detailed work. In keeping with the

PREVIOUS PAGE: *From the windows of his studio-cum-study, Estes can see Central Park; on the easel in equally sharp detail is* The View from Twin Peaks, San Francisco, 1991. ABOVE: *The ziggurat pattern of beautifully grained storage cabinets is a nod to the 1934 Rietveld Zig Zag Chairs encircling the glass table. A composite of early-sixties watercolors by the artist flanks his 1985* Florence, *with a silkscreen on the floor.*

RIGHT: *A Tiffany lamp is reflected on the glass over a Jean Cocteau drawing; Elizabeth King's bronze bust rests atop the foyer cabinet.* OPPOSITE: *A group of Costa Rican pre-Columbian figures assembled on the living room's mirrored table emphasizes the artist's attention to detail, evident in his* Academia, Venice, 1980. *Arshile Gorky's* Staten Island Landscape, 1926, *hangs over the fireplace.*

spirit of the pre-thirties era, Estes designed the inlaid dark and light bird's-eye maple cabinetry in a stepped pattern that reflects Art Deco's merging of fine and applied art. The artist added contemporary curved leather couches in his studio and the living room, period vases with attenuated figures and flowers, and Art Nouveau Tiffany lamps throughout the high-ceilinged *pied-à-terre*.

Modernist paintings by Joseph Stella and Marsden Hartley hang in the living room with an eclectic mix of works by Arshile Gorky, Erte, and Salvador Dali. Pre-Columbian works, all from Costa Rica, make an assemblage on the low, mirrored table, another vignette of organizational skills. Ansel Adams photographs are in the studio-study. In the dining room, works by Luca Giordano, Guiseppe Rivaroli, and Estes are illuminated by a French Art Deco chandelier; its gold gilt is repeated on the elaborate ceiling molding.

Still, the most striking aspect of Estes's apartment is its panoramic view of Central Park, framed by windows in his studio and living room. Against a pale blue sky, buildings along Fifth Avenue are etched in the distance as clearly as in any of Estes's paintings.

A B O V E: *Once a single space, Estes installed a wall of cabinets to create a separate dining room and kitchen. On the kitchen side the ziggurat motif is scaled down to fit the compact space, so skillfully engineered that it can still accommodate a full-size restaurant range and all the accoutrements of a demanding chef.* O P P O S I T E A N D L E F T: *Estes keeps his photo-developing equipment stored in the guest bath, which ingeniously transforms into a darkroom.*

bridging home and art

The practical side of Jan Hashey has always had a deep affection for simple, ordinary, everyday objects. But there is another side, the artist, who sees beyond their mere functionality, finding in their humble shapes the subject matter for her art. Putting a carbon between two sheets of typing paper, Hashey draws her household items life-size with colored felt-tipped markers. All the markings are visible on the carbon copy beneath, showing the "bones of the work." It's a process she describes as "my way of getting rid of some of the clutter in my life." ● Hashey, an alumna of Yale Graduate School, lived for many years in a loft on the edge of SoHo. But by 1989, she felt she needed another venue and wanted more definition between rooms: separate living quarters and studio space. So Hashey and Yasuo Minagawa, a fine-art framer, bought a rambling house

Jan Hashey

high in the Catskill Mountains.

Built in 1887, and set on 106 acres of rolling meadows, woods, and ponds, the seventeen-room house is a typical New York State farmhouse that has been added on to over the years. During the winter months, the couple commutes from New York City on weekends, but for the rest of the year, the farmhouse becomes Hashey's full-time residence. "We fill all eight bedrooms on holidays [her daughter, Jessica Craig-Martin, and son-in-law, Ashley Bickerton, heading the guest list], and my Cuisinart is here," says the artist, who also added a weimaraner, Laredo, son of William Wegman's famed Fay Ray, to the two cats already in residence.

Hashey has a sentimental attachment to her native New England, and that nostalgia is mirrored in the simplicity of her home. Functional objects such as pots and pans hang from a rack in the kitchen, and fireplace tools in the living room take on a sculptural air against the plain white walls. The furniture is a mix of styles, from early American to fifties-era pieces. The library off the master bedroom upstairs is a favorite room, with a folding double card table in heavy maple trimmed in deep red leatherette, carved chairs found at the Salvation Army, and shelves

PREVIOUS PAGE: *The autumnal hues of fallen leaves could have inspired the artist's palette.* ABOVE: *Before heading back to New York City, Hashey's daughter and son-in-law leave a good-bye blackboard note propped on a corner table in the "little kitchen" off the dining room.* OPPOSITE: *There are no extras in Hashey's "big kitchen," everything is to be* *"used up." Whether a collection of brown bowls or a row of painted tins, these unsentimental household goods serve their intended purpose as well as providing subject matter for her drawings.*

crammed with books. Here Hashey and Minagawa can light a fire in the wood-burning stove and watch a movie on the VCR. "What else do you do with guests when it rains?" she asks with a shrug.

A superb cook, Hashey has a big kitchen with French stenciled wallpaper dotted over in paint by a previous artist tenant. In the center of the room is a marble-topped table so massive that it cannot be moved and a resolutely plain-charactered early American sideboard in milky blue paint. An antique stove and a large double sink complete the room, where every object has a place and purpose.

Hashey's recent work is directly influenced by her surroundings, and her studio is housed in a separate wing that can be entered from the back porch, the kitchen, or by a circular staircase leading down from the second-floor balcony. "In the process of personalizing this large house, I became reacquainted with my things, and they suggested to me that they could be useful in my work," says Hashey, who continues to add to the engaging collection of bowls that reinforces this relationship, bridging her art and the objects in her home.

ABOVE AND OPPOSITE: *In her twenty-foot-high studio, Hashey expands her series, "Bowls." Each is drawn to scale, the changes in size creating a movement that makes them appear to dance across the wall. "It's a divine result of the process," she says.* LEFT: *Early risers, the couple takes their morning coffee on the front porch in order to watch the sun rise over the Catskill Mountains.*

ABOVE AND LEFT: *To accentuate the character of the house, Hashey acquired a pine jelly cupboard and a Mission oak table of the same period to enhance the dining room; a collection of candleholders adds to the mood.*
OPPOSITE: *Hashey and Minagawa are avid antiques hunters and world travelers; their furnishings reflect these passions and make an eclectic display in the living room. Above the couch hangs a 1984 Hashey drawing, Flying Wright, named after Russel Wright.*

the rightness of objects

Ed Baynard was a passionate collector of American art pottery long before the compelling shapes of the ceramics emerged in his classical watercolor still lifes. In fact, Baynard didn't begin to paint until he was thirty-one years old. Up to that time, he experimented with various occupations, from sketching for *Women's Wear Daily* to designing posters and costumes for rock stars. "I did not want to be an artist closed off in one room for the rest of my life," says Baynard, whose home, filled to capacity with his pots, is high above the Hudson River, one hundred miles north of New York City. "This seventeen-room house is the result of that experience." ● Built as a summer home in 1905 by Walter van der Bent, chief engineer for the nearby Ashokan Reservoir and engineer for the architecture firm of McKim, Mead, and White, Baynard's house is

Ed Baynard

PREVIOUS PAGE: *The relationship of Baynard's 1986 corroded steel sculpture, Dig, to the land behind his 1905 Arts and Crafts home is emblematic of his desire to link "the pastoral to the architectonic."* LEFT: *Houses of this vintage generally do not have bookcases (or closets), so Baynard, not wishing to disturb its integrity, stacks his gardening catalogues and art books on the floor, adding Tom McKenna's candlesticks on top. He mixes Merrimac, Flameware, and salt-glaze pottery with classic Eileen Gray and Russel Wright furniture in the living room, plus a 1930s screen by Woodstock artist Louise Howard and a 1976 acrylic-on-paper work by Susan Rothenberg.* ABOVE: *This tabletop arrangement of small animal forms is as carefully composed as the artist's watercolors; the lamp and vase are by Fulper.*

a simpler, much taller version of the traditional Arts and Crafts design. The proportions are perfect, but the house is plain, which suits Baynard's minimalist aesthetic. "They didn't gussy it up, as we say in Washington," he remarks. "The house is set to the site; the rooms have the kind of proportion you don't find nowadays. This house feels like a big old house should feel." The rooms are all painted a neutral white to set off his collection of paintings, bric-a-brac, furniture, and, of course, his ceramics. The only exceptions are the blue or subtle gray-mauve guest bedrooms, a concession that complements photographs or paintings hung in these rooms.

A treasured place is the looming tower, accessible only by ladder. From the tower's chestnut-framed windows (the house boasts forty-eight overall), Baynard can see the entire valley and the Ashokan Reservoir. "It is like living in a big tree house," he says. Below are sloping, terraced gardens, and one can see the special placement Baynard has given to his collection of weeping specimen trees: birch, beech, mulberry, pussy willow, and Norwegian spruce. Baynard's large, open studio takes up the entire top floor, once a warren

of servants' rooms, the only signs of which are marks on the floors where walls once stood.

The house is also a repository for Baynard's collection of art and furniture, which, like his own watercolors of flowers, fruit, and vessels, are representations of timeless classicism. Works on paper by Susan Rothenberg, Morris Graves, and Keith Haring exist in harmony with an Eileen Gray table, a Herman Miller table from the fifties, a deep-red lacquered Gerrit Rietveld chair, and one by Russel Wright. Baynard also has furniture of his own design, the most colorful being a glossy yellow plywood long-table supported by sawhorses.

Everywhere, on floors, on tables, on mantels, is his collection of signed pottery: Brauer Flameware, Rookwood, and Niloak to name a few. Baynard points out that his cat, Eliot, has yet to break one. "He's a Maine coon cat. They're not climbers. They walk."

Despite the sheer number of objects, a sense of order prevails: a feeling that the placement of every piece was a decision as important and personal as the arrangements in Baynard's still lifes. "I arrange things this way so that when I walk around in my house, I see what it is all about.

A B O V E : A 1982 James Hanson hangs above Rietveld's 1934 Zig Zag Chair and a 1904 Van Briggle vase. R I G H T : The artist's carved wood Bowls of Fruit, a painted cassette player and speakers, and glass-beaded crafts make a tabletop fantasy garden. O P P O S I T E : William Morris–style wallpaper, original to the house, backdrops a metal-decorated Korean chest-on-chest in the "snuggery," a term borrowed from the cozy Hyde Park room where Eleanor Roosevelt paid bills.

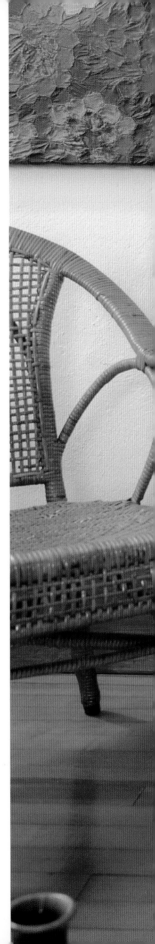

It is very rare that I paint from life; I believe that good objects have a silent life, and I abstract from the object what is really interesting. The idea of the pottery is incorporated into the work, the objects themselves are not. The same with flowers. Composition is inherent. There is a right way to make something that centers you, and centers the people who look at it. It is the rightness of form, and I think that is why most creative people surround themselves with things that remind them of the rightness of objects."

Baynard's life has had many turning points, and he says, "I thought that if I lived long enough, something would happen that met my enthusiasm halfway. Now it seems that life has speeded up, and I've calmed down; it's a good meeting." Nevertheless, this artist never relaxes for very long. "When I was sixteen, I read Delacroix's journals, and he said that to be an artist, you have to be a little one-man band. And I said, 'That's me: That makes sense to me.' "

LEFT: *Whether Baynard walks down the back stairs from his studio to the kitchen, or climbs the ladder to the tower, the fine wood detailing of another era is always present.*

LEFT: *"If I wasn't an artist, I could always get a job as a chef," jokes Baynard about his professionally equipped kitchen.*
ABOVE: *Like Monet's, Baynard's dining room is filled with Japanese prints. "This is a very civilized, grown-up room; a place to dine leisurely in comfortable chairs."*

premier minimalist

Agnes Martin's inspiration springs from her abstract feelings, stirred by the land around her home in Galisteo, New Mexico. "I could paint just as well in New York," Martin says, "but I am better adjusted out here: open spaces, less traffic." Located twenty miles south of Santa Fe, the terrain surrounding her home is flat, with red-clay earth and the snow-capped Sangre de Cristo Mountains looming in the distance. Nearby, excavated Pueblo ruins and cliff dwellings provide destinations for her frequent day trips. ● Martin's unadorned adobe compound is devoid of embellishments so that her mind is free to center on her art. "The life of an artist is completely unmaterialistic," she emphasizes, and she lives simply with only a few mementos, mostly gifts from friends (a hand-woven blanket, wall weavings, small paintings). Flooded with shafts of

Agnes Martin

PREVIOUS PAGE: *A self-sufficient woman, the painter has built numerous adobe structures, including portions of her studio.* RIGHT: *Light streaming through the paned windows of Martin's home echoes the subtle grids of her canvases.* BELOW: *The prairie grasses surrounding the house "quiver in light and bend and break in silence," says Martin. As in her paintings, her concern is less for nature than for expression.* OPPOSITE: *"I recommend to collectors that they hang my paintings in the bedroom so when they wake, before daily cares strike, they can have the experience of responding to the abstract," says Martin, whose studio rocker faces a canvas in progress.*

light, the combined kitchen-dining-living room is furnished with a comfortable muted pastel sofa, table and chairs, and two high-backed spindled rockers facing a carved wooden statue of Moses that stands before the large picture window.

Agnes Martin was born in 1912 in Saskatchewan, Canada, and came to New York to study and paint when she was twenty. However, not until she was almost fifty years old did she develop and paint her legendary grid variations, which juxtapose horizontal bands and lines over pale fields of meditative, floating colors.

Although the artist is eighty, she seems to have eluded age. Small and robust with white cropped hair and fine skin, she laughs easily, as if she has truly found her own path to serenity. "A painter should try to apply the line of Wordsworth, 'emotion recollected in tranquillity,'" she maintains. That credo and her "surrender of the life of the intellect to the life of inspiration" is evident in her life as well as her art, which encapsulates memories of moments of perfection and freedom from the cares of this world.

aRTISTS HAVE TYPICALLY RE-

treated from their home bases for

reasons and destinations as varied

as their work. Some search for new

visions, like George Grosz, who

left Berlin to fulfill his dreams in

A cottage hideaway in Connecticut's rolling hills is home to Carol Anthony.

America, or Georgia O'Keeffe, who found hers in New Mex-

ico. German Expressionist Paul Kleinschmidt departed for

The Home as

Arles, France, a landscape well known for its effect on artistic

thinking. For today's artists, a retreat is also an alternate

way of living away from the fast pace of the art world.

Because of the deep concentration required to produce a work of art and the social demands put on an artist these days, it is hardly surprising that the artist might wish to escape the city and go a bit farther afield, if only for a few summer months. When the local people describe the part of New York's Delaware County where Tom and Claire Wesselmann have their getaway as "the boondocks," it makes Claire laugh because that is precisely why the ecology-minded couple spends their

Retreat summers there.

To the north, Alex Katz thinks of his yellow frame house in Maine primarily as a place to paint, but he and his wife, Ada, also enjoy entertaining friends who drop by or stay awhile. Sometimes the retreat in the wilderness is a full-time residence and a commitment to self-sufficiency. Neil Welliver and his artist wife, Shelia Geoffrion, live in Maine year-round; when

High color enlivens Larry Bell's 200-year-old adobe home in Taos.

Welliver closes his "shop" in the evening, time is given over to family, dining on fish from their ponds and vegetables and fruit from their organic garden. The weekend retreat can be the solution for artists who want to be able to travel back and forth from a city at a moment's notice. On Thursday or Friday, collaborators David McDermott and Peter McGough head for their dilapidated,

Grained cabinetry was crafted by Laddie John Dill for his Santa Monica bedroom.

unheated, early nineteenth-century house in Oak Hill, New York, to enjoy rides in their horse-drawn buggy and to set the stage for what they call "time-traveling." Though Lowell Nes-

The sculpture park setting of Anthony Caro's studio-home in upstate New York.

bitt may only spare a few days a week from his New York studio, he looks forward to work in the gardens that surround his secluded stone house. And some, like Helen Frankenthaler, need

A wooden deck and lanai make Dill's pool area a peaceful oasis.

never leave the city at all to find a peaceful enclave. Still, whether urban or rural, the home as retreat is a place for quiet contemplation, privacy, and simple pleasures, a place to renew the artistic spirit.

By preserving, recording, and observing the fast-disappearing landscape in their art as well as in their environment, painters Neil Welliver and Shelia Geoffrion have made a commitment to living in harmony with nature. Neil Welliver says, "My proudest achievement in this environment is not to have screwed around with it. I just let it take care of itself. It's the whole configuration that pleases me, not just one thing." To understand the geography and climate of the terrain, its light and stillness, one need only to refer to Welliver's confrontational, highly detailed paintings: "One of the reasons I came to Maine and decided to stay was that I could look from here to that mountain over there. That's a mile and a half or so—extremely crystalline as far as you can see," he says. ● In 1975, the artist's first house

Neil Welliver/
Shelia Geoffrion

burned down in an electrical fire. Rather than build from scratch, Welliver found a compound of old buildings for sale in the nearby woods, and hired a crew, including local boat builders, to move them, piece by piece, to the foundation of his original home. First the cellar was rebuilt with rocks dug from a neighbor's field. Then Welliver, a perfectionist to the last detail, spent the next year restoring every square foot of the main house and attached studio barn, which are joined together to make one continuous building, as is typical of early New England farmhouses. Using elements salvaged from another house of similar vintage that was slated for demolition to replace original timberwork and missing pieces, Welliver replicated his old house, even replacing windows with old glass. Today, with the exception of a skylight in Welliver's studio at the end of this 140-foot-long structure, the house looks as it might have in the early nineteenth century: its weathered spruce siding silvered with age.

Born in Washington, D.C., but raised in Central America, Shelia Geoffrion Welliver at first found winters in Maine difficult. Now, completely acclimated, the artist goes

PREVIOUS PAGE: The colors of autumn are even more vivid against the formal simplicity of the aged front door. RIGHT: A sentinel of birdhouses edges the Wellivers' one-acre organic garden. Down the road is the building housing Shelia's studio. BELOW: A close-knit group of artists, writers, filmmakers, and lawyers often gathers at the Welliver table to dine on lobster, moose, and homegrown seasonal vegetable treats. OPPOSITE: Bowls and baskets hold ripened produce from their garden.

outside to paint and to discover new plants to incorporate in her work. Shelia likes to cook with the ingredients taken from the big garden that supplies most of their produce. ("I'm sort of her helper," says Welliver, "but everything around here is pretty much a collaboration.") Trout are caught in one of the ponds, and Araucana chickens from Chile supply multicolored, pastel eggs. To complete this picture of self-sufficiency, a windmill generates all the Wellivers' electricity.

Neil Welliver, a no-nonsense man who thinks nothing of tramping out to paint in the woods when the snow is a foot deep and the temperature is well below freezing, started spending summers in Maine in the late fifties and eventually bought a house on 106 acres near Lincolnville. Welliver admits, "A friend got me off the pavement and onto the dirt roads." By the early seventies, he had accumulated 1,500 acres. He says he

LEFT: *Neil Welliver's formalist training (he studied under Josef Albers at Yale) is apparent in the 16,000-square-foot interior of the house, where the stark black-white theme of the living room is enlivened by the richness of the Shaker-red painted doors and trim, the pre-Columbian figures, and a nineteenth-century mahogany apothecary cabinet.*

LEFT: *In the bedroom a sponge-painted desk shares a corner with a papier-mâché washtub.*
BELOW: *Neil Welliver transposes the Shaker idiom to his own finely crafted built-in drawers complete with pegged pulls. His 1991 painting rests on the mantel.*
OPPOSITE: *The porch, overlooking the expansive fields, is a warm-weather haven; a door at one end leads to a cozy guest bedroom. Atop a cabinet near the bedroom door is Shelia's 1985 painting,* Window.

is "more interested in the formal aspects than in just copying what's out there. In any given forest situation, there are things being born, maturing, dying, dead, and decaying. Once you accept yourself as part of the environment, then you and the trees and the animals and so on become one. There is a continuum, and you don't separate elements. It makes you see it very differently."

The interior of the Welliver home is commodious and often scattered with books and crossword puzzles, two Welliver obsessions. Though most of the original furniture was destroyed in the fire, the rooms are now filled with comfortable, unpretentious pieces. The almost Shaker-like simplicity and calm order in the rooms is an antidote to the turbulent, light-splintered natural world of Welliver's canvases just outside.

It takes energy to live like Neil Welliver, painting seven days a week, "ten to five like a shopkeeper without stopping. But if I'm painting in the woods, it's all determined by the sun." Every season offers new possibilities: "If you go out and just muse, walk around and let things come upon you, it's remarkable what's out there that you otherwise might not see. Just let it appear. That's really the key to the church."

urban classic

Following a visit to Jackson Pollock's studio and a sojourn in Nova Scotia in 1952, Helen Frankenthaler spread a canvas across her studio floor, thinned down her oil paints, and began to pour. The result, a merging of landscape-like shapes in stains of gentle color, became *Mountains and Sea*. This seminal painting changed the prevailing style of the time and laid the groundwork for the color field movement. "My ideas," the artist says, "come from many sources: my feelings about landscape, paintings from the past, all kinds of experience. I start to work and let it develop." ● From that time, Frankenthaler has become a legend and has also survived a generation of artists known for their excesses. The Upper East Side town house that has been her home since 1957 is as balanced and contemplative as her paintings. And per the words of

Helen Frankenthaler

Yeats, who wrote, "The intellect of man must choose perfection of the life or of the work," Frankenthaler has chosen to make a distinction between her art and her home. "In art, I strive for a beautiful working order, often made from chaos," she says, "but I want to make it very clear that there is a tremendous difference between one's art and one's interior design. For example, there will probably always be a permanent chaos in my night table drawer or in my cellar. There are areas that don't work properly. I want perfection in my work and should not expect to achieve it in my environment."

Nevertheless, Frankenthaler's home is altogether urbane and serene. Though the entire house has been renovated ("slowly, from top to bottom"), its 120-year-old character has been left relatively undisturbed. Frankenthaler feels, "You can't make too many radical changes to the original spine or shell of the house, or you might risk damaging its original intentions." Other than some structural changes, the only additions were personal touches, "the unusual mixed with a kind of classic. The classic with surprises." Among these unexpected differences are the artist's favorite tiles placed at random, and a specially built terrace off the bedroom

allows Frankenthaler the urban luxury of privacy outdoors, complete with a view of the fruit-bearing pear tree in her neighbor's garden below. Walls throughout the four-story brownstone are liberally covered with an eclectic blend of works of art.

On a platform at the front of the living room is the solarium, an intimate nook burgeoning with plants and tapestry-covered couches: a startling contrast to the green-tubed Le Corbusier furniture just beyond. In the dining room, in addition to the oversized Georgian table and contemporary chairs, are two made-to-order chairs that "just fit my back. I designed them. They are outrageously, wonderfully different, and in them you can have supper for two overlooking the garden."

But perhaps the real heart of the house is the large kitchen, and its table is the center of activity. A bright red stove stands between the cobalt blue and jet black cabinets, and the floor tiles and ceiling panels are in varying shades of ochre.

Frankenthaler likes to entertain. "I think artists enjoy the company of others. What matters is to make them feel welcome and at ease. For me, the most important features of a house are growth, change, comfort, endurance, and of course, visual pleasure."

ABOVE: *A rounded marble-topped island separates the living room from the solarium with its bump-out steel-and-glass bay window that sheds additional light on the parlor floor.* OPPOSITE: *Frankenthaler has surrounded her Georgian table with contemporary chairs on casters (they also tilt). "The dining room [which she calls "Tree Tops"] is one of the most useful rooms in the house; a great place for doing desk work or large projects," says the artist, whose 1989 acrylic on canvas painting, Star Gazing, spans the east wall.*

glacial river bed into a pond where he grows exotic grasses, ferns, iris, and corkscrew willows. "A natural channel already existed, so I brought in a backhoe and shoveled the dirt up on both sides. There were rocks on two sides, so I dammed up the two ends."

The most recent addition to Nesbitt's property is a pyramid. But Nesbitt, who had always been interested in Egyptology, wanted a pyramid that would contain an indoor pool, a studio area, a dining room, a loft, and a garage while affording plenty of wall space for his paintings. "When I realized that putting a swimming pool in the pyramid would take up too much floor space, I had Phillips design a ten-foot-square subway grating to go over the pool, so you could actually swim underneath the dining room. Not that I've had one meal at that table. I swim there and I draw," says the artist, who also installed an elaborate stereo system. "The acoustics are incredible, but I prefer to listen to the pool filter."

ABOVE AND RIGHT: *Irises are Nesbitt's trademark; in the bedroom are watercolors, silkscreens, and paintings of this signature image along with a 1988 portrait of his English Mastiff, Stoneleigh. A jacket taken from his collection of camouflage clothing hangs in the dressing room. "I think of them as art objects," says the artist, who dubs them "art camo" when he wears the garb to work.*

RIGHT: *Nesbitt's bronze Antherium, 1979, rests atop the table in the pyramid. The 1927 Mies chairs were wrapped in truck inner tubes by Tim Hoffman.*

sculptures to his collection of sculpted three-dimensional ceramic fruits, vegetables, and flowers to dog collars and pillows with needle-pointed homilies.

Nesbitt grew up in a Baltimore suburb called Stoneleigh (as is his English mastiff), but that is not the only reason he chose the same name for his home. "In Putnam County it is almost impossible to put a shovel or even a trowel into the earth and not hit a stone. It makes gardening very, very difficult. Frequently, you run into what is known as 'ledge.' You are then talking big stones." Instead of fighting nature, Nesbitt and his architect, Preston Phillips, decided to work with it, constructing the house directly on top of the ledge and on terraced levels that follow the slope of the land. "It took three cases of dynamite to put in the footings," says the artist.

Not only did they use rock quarried from Nesbitt's property for the floors and walls, slabs of stone form a natural stairway bridging the foyer, kitchen, dining area, and living room. To acknowledge the source of all this stone, he exposed the ledge beneath the house, adding a gentle waterfall to aerate the exotic plants that border it.

Despite the rocky terrain, Nesbitt created gardens and turned a now-dry

ABOVE: *In a compact galley kitchen, Nesbitt combines glossy dark green cabinetry with light butcher-block counters, then suspends brightly colored mugs from a rack in the center. His 1966 Three Yellow Iris on Gold hangs on the adjacent wall.* LEFT: *Stone-topped cabinets holding fanciful platters of ceramic flowers and vegetables face subway grating in another guise, here used for a tabletop.*

PREVIOUS PAGE:
Asphalt-over-wood
supports comprise the
exterior walls of the
pyramid, which
features a one-way
mirrored pyramidion
at its top; inside, the
walls are painted gold.
A "rock-sculpture
landscape" just outside
the main entrance to
the house is part of an
ongoing project with
James Sullivan.
RIGHT: *Nesbitt says*
his paintings represent
"the voice of all
nature," and the living
room reflects the
elements of earth, air,
water, and fire. Blue
Sheet, *1973, hangs over*
the fireplace; tiny
spotlights illuminate
his 1967 Iris I, *left;*
Three Iris, *1970, right.*

elemental geometry

Imagine a lively dialogue between art, stones, ponds, flowers, dogs, and geometric shapes, and you have a pretty good picture of Lowell Nesbitt's country house: a setting of gardens with cascading flows of water, his trademark irises blooming beside a rock sculpture, a walled garden enclosing a mammoth boulder, and much more, all in perfect synchronization with Nesbitt's art. ● Inside, the house is dominated by Nesbitt's large canvases of oversized flowers (self-contained gardens in catalogue-bright colors), favorite dogs, and nudes. Nesbitt considers the circle, the square, and the triangle the basic shapes of nature, and these forms recur again and again in both his work and in his house. Tiny spotlights illuminate the seemingly endless array of objects and works of art that cover every available surface, from his own flower

Lowell Nesbitt

features in Katz's paintings of colorful landscapes, figures, and houses executed with suppressed brushwork and no extraneous detail, the house's interior is simple and spare. The walls are in pastel hues, contrasting with the blue and red checkered floor tiles and vivid-colored trim in the hall. Three straight rockers and a small turn-of-the-century sofa are in the living room, with a few of the artist's older works on the walls. Off this room is a pale lilac-pink study with a rectangular grand piano and a desk.

Cadmium yellow has always been one of Katz's favorite colors, and both the living room and the exterior of the house are in similar shades of this bright color. "We tried different colors in this room, then we finally got the yellow all over, and it looked right. It's been the same color for twenty years," says Katz. And the word "right" has a certain resonance when spoken by Katz, a painter who chooses his words as carefully as his palette.

LEFT: *In the spartan kitchen, planes of high-tone color are a nod to the artist's well-known unembellished style.*

BELOW: *First masking the hand-hewn beams and wood crossbars, Katz had polyurethane sprayed on the walls for insulation in this former barn-studio turned dining-workroom. A poster reproduces a painting of Ada, the artist's wife and the model for more than a hundred images.* RIGHT: *The "Yellow House" is easily recognizable from many of Katz's canvases.*

PREVIOUS PAGE: *Known for his sleek, hard-edged canvases, Katz allows some painted surfaces in his home to remain surprisingly rough.* ABOVE: *The artist, who studied at Cooper Union, exhibits an early work, 1952; a peek into a bedroom reveals his circa-1960 Ada Reclining.* OPPOSITE: *In the yellow living room, Katz strips away* the inessentials, *encouraging a dialogue between the objects and the space they occupy. Behind the Victorian sofa hangs a 1972 Joseph Cornell color gravure;* The Dog, *a 1978 aquatint by Katz, is at right. A flattened spoon portrait by William King shares the mantel with Katz's carved limestone head and a miniature pipe-stand armchair found in a Lincolnville shop.*

ocean," says Katz, who prefers the climate inland, where the lush landscape becomes nearly tropical during the summer months. "It's warm during the day and cool at night. We're separated from the ocean by hills, which keep out the fog. And visually, it was open, too." By cutting back the trees and "civilizing" the land, Katz exposed the meadows that surround his wood-frame home, a former rum house built at least 175 years ago and moved to its present foundation on Slab City Road in the early 1900s. Both the house and the attached barn are supported by their original hand-hewn beams.

A few basic improvements were made: Plumbing was installed, a dormer was added for extra space, the woodshed was remodeled into a proper kitchen, and Katz's former studio barn was designated the dining room. Since the Katzes return to New York in early September, the fireplace provides all the heat they need on chilly nights. Throughout the house the wide-board floors are kept bare, polished with age. Katz has built a new studio that overlooks the lake and is obscured from the house by a dense pine forest. "I like a beautiful studio, and the things around me to be kind of peaceful," Katz says.

Like the straightforward, unadorned

stylized simplicity

Alex Katz is a keen observer of attitude, of style, and his life and paintings reflect the values of a native New Yorker: a sense of theater, a love of movies, an interest in literature and dance. But every June the painter and his wife, Ada, forsake their SoHo loft and the heat and noise of the city for their retreat in rural Maine. It is here that Katz creates paintings that translate ordinary sights into his unique style of realism: cinematic wide-angle views and close-ups that are ripe with symbols. ● "The light here is very different, it changes abruptly, and that's the reason I'm here," says Katz, who was introduced to Maine during the summers of 1949 and 1950 as a student at the Skowhegan School of Painting and Sculpture. In 1953, Katz bought this house in Lincolnville, three miles from the coast. "I like the ocean, but I didn't want to live *on* the

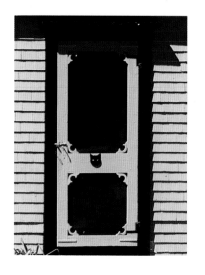

Alex Katz

Every weekend David McDermott and Peter McGough leave their studio in Brooklyn and journey back through time to Tripp House, their Federal-style home in Oak Hill, New York. With its interiors in a state of semi-decay, the colors warmed and gentled by age, Tripp House appears like a series of old still lifes. These rustic, serene tableaus both inspire and reflect the vision of nineteenth-century life that informs the pair's jointly executed canvases and photographs. ● Built in 1800, Tripp House has been left virtually unchanged since 1888. It has no electricity, telephone, or plumbing; water is drawn from a hand-dug well near the back door and heated in a kettle in the fireplace for tea or bathing. On the walls peeling plaster, paint, and wallpaper reveal layers of milky color. All this suits McDermott and

David McDermott/
Peter McGough

PREVIOUS PAGE: *Time seems to stand still in McDermott and McGough's Federal-style house, the tranquil tableau brought to life only by the vivid colors of fresh produce.* RIGHT: *Tripp House's sober exterior.* BELOW: *After jaunts in their horse-drawn antique buggy, the collaborators return to their spots before the ever-burning fire, not only their source of heat, but also the place for cooking.* OPPOSITE: *Old wallpaper and a birdcage perched above a library cabinet holding fustian books turn this scene back two centuries.*

McGough perfectly. Impeccably dressed in Edwardian attire, they spend their days at Tripp House almost exactly as the original owners might have.

On a typical weekend, McDermott tends the outdoors while McGough does the cooking. (The artists are vegetarians and eat only natural foods.) Their colleague, Jeffrey Gasparini, whose family owned Tripp House in the late 1800s and who edits their periodical, *The Cottage*, looks after the antique buggies, the horse, and stable in the back. When the weather is fine the entire household goes for a ride in an immaculate 1913 Model-T Ford, with Gasparini, properly outfitted in livery, serving as driver. They are often accompanied by their dogs: Damon, a dachschund; Diogenes, a springer spaniel; and Julius Salernius, a Brittany spaniel.

All of the furniture in Tripp House dates from the eighteenth and nineteenth centuries, and much of it is chipped and worn, but McDermott and McGough prefer their dilapidated belongings to perfect antiques. These objects, they claim, with their patina of age, are more conducive to "time traveling."

They also own the white clapboard general store next door, which once belonged to the Tripp family

LEFT: *McGough calls their work "advertisements for the past." McDermott says, "For our art, it is just a matter of photographing our life."* BELOW LEFT: *This staircase leading to a bedroom above the pantry could be an image for one of their photographs.* BELOW: *Hallway linoleum is patterned after Oriental carpeting.* OPPOSITE: *Wearing antique clothes and shirts with high starched collars, the artists "time-travel" to recapture the grace of an era gone by, taking high tea in the dining room with cracked, but prized, porcelain.*

and which presently houses their collections of "notions," such as Chinese toothbrushes made with real bristle, oil lamps, wicker bird cages, pewters and porcelains, even wooden toy soldiers. "Some of the things are new," says Gasparini, "but they're old-fashioned."

To visit the partners is to experience a time when life was harder but simpler and, to their minds, a good deal better. The artists take a dim view of commercialism, waste, overconsumption, the planned obsolescence of this era, and anything plastic. Unlike Oscar Wilde, who said, "I put my talent in my work and my genius in my life," McDermott and McGough feel the two are inseparable; by surrounding themselves with artifacts from the past, they firmly believe they are living more artistic lives. But truthfully the two men thoroughly enjoy their chosen lifestyle. It takes a great deal of courage, confidence, and conviction to maintain this level of adherence to their ideals, and they have succeeded with grace, charm, and without a hint of irony.

lessons in ecology

Tom Wesselmann's series of over-scale paintings of "The Great American Nude" became emblematic of the Pop art movement, but it is the barns and trees that surround his summer home in Delaware County, New York, that have inspired the laser-cut steel landscape paintings he has been exhibiting since 1989. "I always wanted to do land-scapes, but I couldn't find a way in," Wesselmann says. "I was overwhelmed by all those trees; all those leaves. Then I started looking across the lake with my binoculars out of focus, and that simplified everything. It broke down the landscape into natural patterns. So I drew the images that I saw." ● When Wesselmann and his wife, Claire, a graphic designer, bought their property in 1970, it was because Wesselmann had always dreamed of having his own lake. "It was a bullhead lake when I got it. So I put

T o m   W e s s e l m a n n

PREVIOUS PAGE: *An avid fisherman, Wesselmann attempted to turn the lake into a haven for bass, which proved to be a huge ecological undertaking.* RIGHT: *The natural setting influenced the architectural decisions the couple made about their house: "Tom thought the ultimate success would be if he could go across the lake, look back, and not be able to find it," says Claire. The table was crafted from stone quarried on the property long ago.*

bass in, and resolved not to fish for five years; then I would have the kind of fishing that men only dream of." Unfortunately, Wesselmann soon found he had unwittingly altered the ecosystem of his lake. "The bass ate everything: all the bullheads, the minnows, the frogs, the salamanders."

Wesselmann reclaimed overgrown meadows and bought an almost-noiseless electric tractor to maintain them. This project provided ecology lessons in that while some species of trees and wildlife flourished, others did not. The artist learned to live with the deer eating most of his corn, which he had planted in a serpentine pattern. Other animals chewed the fruit trees right down to the ground. To keep the beavers from jamming the dam at the end of the lake, he designed a new spillway like a long sloping drive.

By the time the Wesselmanns decided to renovate and enlarge their house four years later, they were happy to collaborate with nature. Tearing out all but the original stone walls that now enclose the living-dining room, the couple added bedrooms and bathrooms using materials indigenous to the area. Hard maple was used for most of the interior walls and hemlock for parts of the outside facing, with large

windows to overlook the lake.

These days, Wesselmann is more likely to be found working than fishing. "My ideal is not to lift one finger except to paint, draw, and write some music," says the artist, who is also a prolific country music composer. "That's all I want to do . . . and mow a little grass. That's it."

ABOVE AND RIGHT: *All but the exterior stone walls were torn down; now the original stone backdrops the kitchen island or is a departure point for the additions.* OVERLEAF: *Tag-sale "finds" often become images in Tom Wesselmann's work.*

artists' information and representatives

Peter Alexander
Born 1939, Los Angeles, CA
James Corcoran Gallery,
Santa Monica, CA

Stephen Antonakos
Born 1926, Agios Nikolaos,
Laconia, Greece

Arman
Born 1928, Nice, France
Marisa del Rey Gallery,
New York City

Charles Arnoldi
Born 1946, Dayton, OH
Fred Hoffman Gallery,
Santa Monica, CA
Charles Cowles Gallery,
New York City

Ed Baynard
Born 1940, Washington, D.C.

Lynda Benglis
Born 1941, Lake Charles, LA
Paula Cooper Gallery,
New York City

Billy Al Bengston
Born 1934, Dodge City, KS
James Corcoran Gallery,
Santa Monica, CA

Mel Bochner
Born 1940, Pittsburgh, PA
Sonnabend Gallery,
New York City

David Deutsch
Born 1943, Los Angeles, CA
Blum Helman Gallery,
New York City

Richard Estes
Born 1932, Keewanee, IL
Allan Stone Gallery,
New York City

Helen Frankenthaler
Born 1928, New York City, NY
André Emmerich Gallery,
New York City

Shelia Geoffrion
Born 1955, Washington, D.C.

Nancy Graves
Born 1940, Pittsfield, MA
M. Knoedler & Co.,
New York City

Jan Hashey
Born 1938, Boston, MA
Barbara Toll Gallery
New York City

Alex Katz
Born 1927, Brooklyn, NY
Marlborough Gallery,
New York City
Robert Miller Gallery,
New York City

Lizbeth Marano
Born 1950, Newark, NJ

Agnes Martin
Born 1912, Saskatchewan, Can.
Pace Gallery,
New York City

David McDermott
Born 1952, Hollywood, CA
Sperone Westwater,
New York City

Peter McGough
Born 1958, Syracuse, NY
Sperone Westwater,
New York City

Nabil Nahas
Born 1950, Beirut, Lebanon

Lowell Nesbitt
Born 1933, Baltimore, MD

Izhar Patkin
Born 1956, Haifa, Israel
Holly Solomon Gallery,
New York City

Tavlos
Born 1944, Alton, IL
Presden Gallery,
Santa Fe, NM

Neil Welliver
Born 1929, Millville, PA
Marlborough Gallery,
New York City

Tom Wesselmann
Born 1931, Cincinnati, Ohio
Sidney Janis Gallery,
New York City
International Images,
New York City

index